Samsung Galaxy A32 5G for Seniors

A Complete Guide to Master the new Samsung Galaxy A32 5G for Seniors

Nelly A. Robbins

Contents

INTRODUCTION 1
Chapter 1: Device Layout 3
Chapter 2 Start Using Your Device 6
Chapter 3: Navigation 17
Chapter 4: Home Screen Customization 27
Chapter 5: Notification panel 39
Chapter 6: Enter text 51
Chapter 7: Using Apps 71
Chapter 8: Contacts 96
Chapter 9: Phone 112
Chapter 10: Messages 140
Chapter 11: Google apps 146
Chapter 12: Camera 154
Chapter 13: Gallery 173
Chapter 14: Multi-window 185
Chapter 15: Settings 188
Chapter 16: Sounds and vibration 220
Chapter 17: Notifications 233
Chapter 18: Display 240
Chapter 19: Lock Screen and Security 253
Chapter 20: Accounts 274
Chapter 21: Device Maintenance 279
Chapter 22: Accessibility 305

Chapter 23: Edge panels............................ 321
Index.. 327

INTRODUCTION

Samsung galaxy a32 comes with a compact design with unique camera bumps at the back. With an attractive display, the a32 offers 6.4 inches in diagonal, and a proper Samsung Super AMOLED SCREEN.

You also get a 1080p resolution and a fast 90 hertz refresh rate. Of course, this is opposed to the 720p lcd with a standard refresh rate that you get on the a32. Even though the bezels are a bit thick here, you have a U shaped notch cut out, eating a bit of screen space.

In cpu and gpu benchmark, the scores are at the bottom of the chart. The phone isn't exactly slow, but we have seen better performance in the competition. And even though the 90 hertz refresh rate does have some smoothness.

The good news is that it holds the new Android 11 software. Meaning, some of the new features introduced in the new Samsung OneUI software are included also in this device.

The truth of the matter is that there's a whole bunch of features embedded in the new Samsung Galaxy a32 that can be very useful to you. In this guide, we have included all of the features and how to master each and every one of them with ease. So get started now by reading through this guide today.

Chapter 1: Device Layout

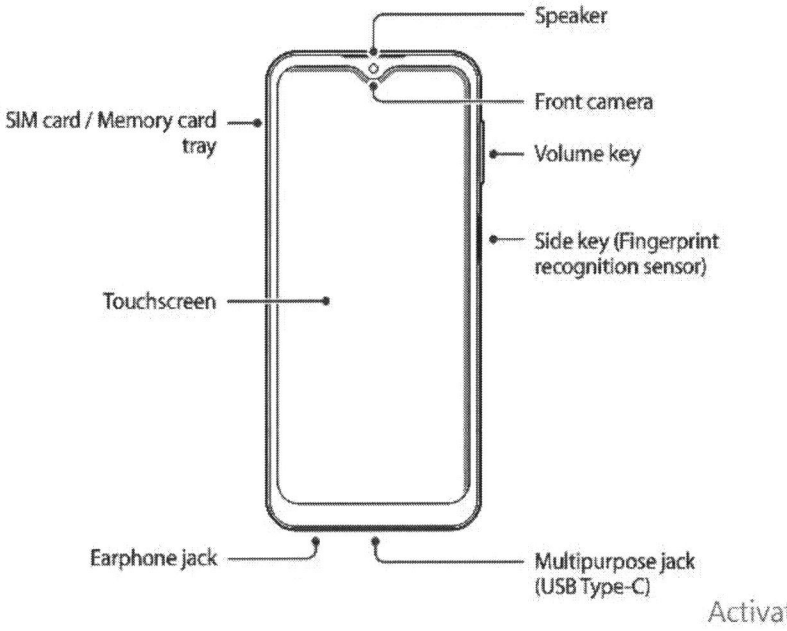

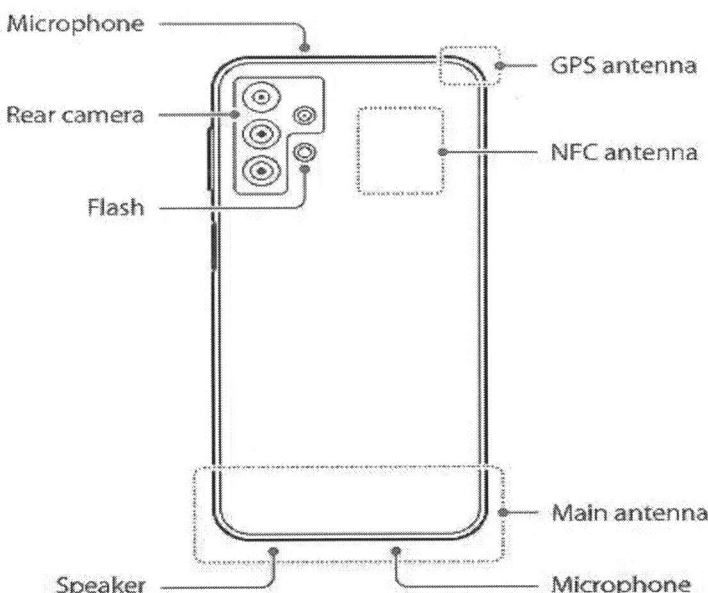

Your device makes use of a nano-SIM card, though there may be a preinstalled SIM card. There may also be the option to make use of your own SIM card. For accurate information, contact your carrier.

💡 Note that there are local and federal laws guiding the use of mobile gadgets on a ship or aircraft. Therefore, ensure that you check for and follow instructions from the appropriate authority on how to use your device.

💡 Note that Samsung sells the wall chargers separately. Only make use of the Samsung-approved cables and chargers to avoid device damage or injury. Also, avoid using damaged, incompatible or worn-out batteries, cables, and chargers. Your warranty may be voided if you make use of other batteries and chargers.

💡 Note that your device has an IP68 rating for water and dust resistance. To maintain this resistance feature, ensure that the openings of the SIM card tray are kept water and dust-free. Also, ensure that the tray is inserted before any liquid exposure.

Chapter 2 Start Using Your Device

Boot your device

Turn on your device with the Side key. If the body of the device is broken or cracked, do not make use of it.

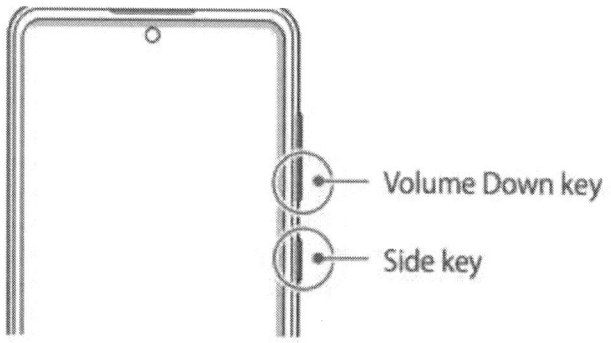

○ Boot the phone by holding down the Side key.

• To switch off, hold down the Volume down and Side keys simultaneously, then tap ⏻ Power off. Tap Confirm when you are prompted.

• To restart, hold down the Volume Down and Side buttons simultaneously, then tap ⊙ Restart. Tap Confirm when you are prompted.

💡 Navigate to Advanced features > Side key > How to power off your phone to know more about device power off via Settings ⊙.

Use the Setup Wizard

When you boot your phone for the first time, the Setup Wizard will guide you through the details of how to set up your device.

Follow the instructions for language selection, Wi-Fi connection, account setup, location service selection, knowing more about the features of your device, and others.

Data Transfer from an old Device

Make use of the Smart Switch™ to transfer music, videos, contacts, calendars, notes, messages, etc. from your old device. The Smart Switch feature allows you to do this transfer via Wi-Fi, USB cable, or a computer.

1. Navigate to Settings > ⊙ Accounts and backup > Bring data from the old device.

2. Follow the instruction and choose the content for transfer.

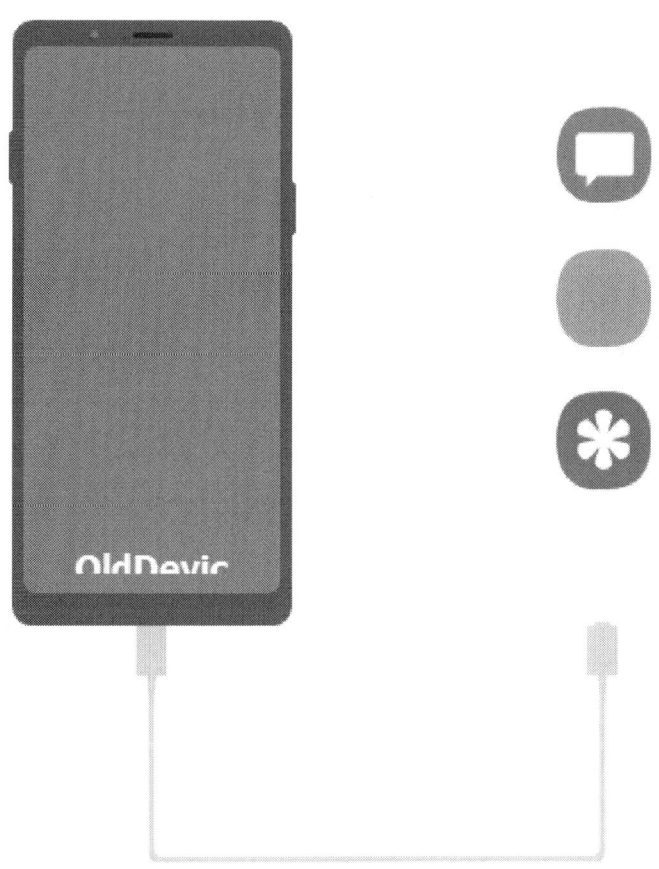

Device Locking and Unlocking

Make use of the screen lock feature of your phone to secure it. Set the screen time of the phone to lock automatically.

Side key settings

You can modify the shortcuts of the Side key.

Double press

Select the feature that will be launched when you press the Side key twice.

1. Navigate to Settings > ⚙ Advanced features > Side key.
2. Activate this feature by tapping Double press, then tap any of the options:
- Quick launch camera (default)
- Open app
- Open Bixby

Press and Hold

Choose the feature that is launch when you press and hold down the side Key.

1. Go to Settings > ⚙ Advanced

features > Side key.

2. Then Tap any of the following options that is placed under the Press and hold menu:

- Wake Bixby (default)
- Power off menu

Accounts

You will have to configure and manage your accounts.

☼ Be aware that Accounts may support contacts, calendars, email, and other features. To know more, contact your carrier.

Add a Google Account

Sign in to your Google Account to gain access to your account-installed apps, Google Cloud Storage, and also make use of all the Android™ features of your device.

1. Navigate to Settings > ⊚ Accounts and backup > Manage accounts.

2. Tap ✚ Add

Note that the Factory Reset Protection (FRP) will be activated when you sign in to your Google Account. The FRP requires that you provide your Google Account info before you can perform a factory reset.

Add a Samsung Account

Sign in to your Samsung account to get access to exclusive Samsung content and also be able to use Samsung apps.

○ Navigate to Settings > Samsung

account.

Add an Outlook account

Sign in to your Outlook® account to see and manage your mails.

1. Navigate to Settings > Accounts and backup > Manage accounts.

2. Tap Add account > Outlook.

Set up voicemail

When you first access your voicemail service, you can also set it up. You can access it via the Phone app. Depending on the carrier, the options may differ.

1. Navigate to Phone, and hold down the 1 key or press Voicemail.

2. Follow the prompt for password creation, greeting recording, and also name recording.

Battery Charging

A rechargeable battery powers your device. Also included is a reversible Type C USB cable. You can make use of this cable on smartphones, USB Type-C travel adapter, laptops, wireless and portable charging both for data transfer and charging.

☼ Be aware that the charger may become hot when charging the device and even stop charging. This is a normal operation occurrence and does not affect the performance or lifespan of the device. Simply unplug the charger and allow the device to cool. Visit samsung.com/us/support/answer/ANS00076952 to know more.

Wired Charging

You have to connect the USB cable to the USB power adaptor and have the cable plugged into the devices.

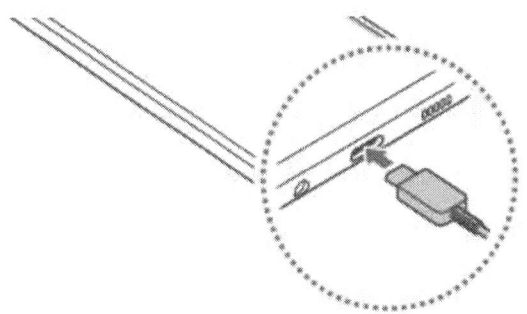

Quick charging

1. Open the Settings app, and then tap Battery and device care → Battery → More battery settings, and then have any of the feature activated.

• **Fast charging:** If you want to use the fast charging feature, then utilizing a battery charger that works adaptive fast charging.

Even if the screen is turned off, you can charge the battery rapidly.

Chapter 3: Navigation

The touch screen of your phone responds best when touched lightly using a capacitive stylus or your finger. You may damage the screen if you use a metallic object or excessive force. The warranty does not cover this damage.

Tap

Touch items lightly to either launch or select them.

- Select an item by tapping it.
- Zoom an image in or out by double-tapping it.

Swipe

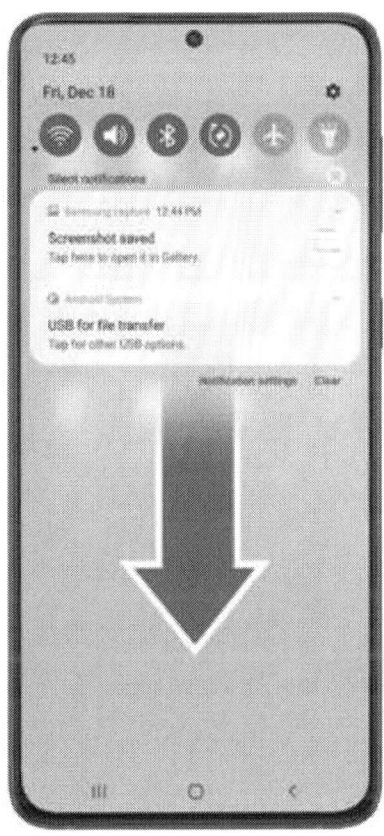

Drag your fingers lightly across the screen.

- To unlock the device, swipe the screen.
- To scroll through the menu options or

the Home screen, swipe the screen.

Drag and drop

Hold down an item and move it to another location.

- Add the shortcut for an app by dragging it.
- Drag a widget to move it to another location.

Zoom in and out

You will have to bring out your forefinger and thumb on the screen apart or together to zoom in and out.

- If you want to zoom out, move your forefinger and thumb on the screen together.
- You will have to move your forefinger and thumb apart on the screen to zoom in.

Touch and hold

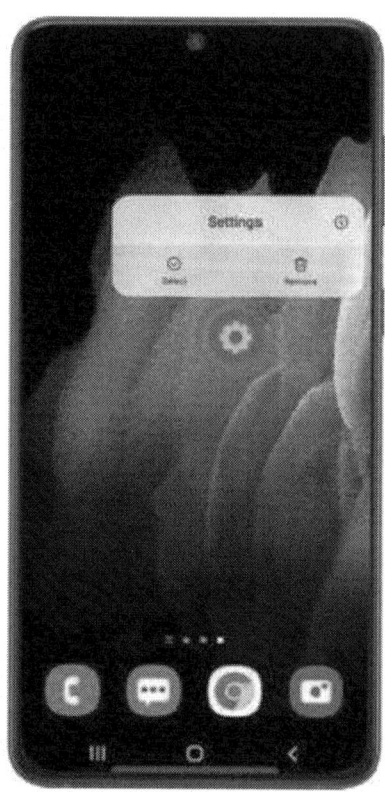

Activate items by touching and holding the

- Show a pop-up menu option by touching and holding a field.
- To customize your Home screen, touch and hold it.

Navigation bar

Use either the full-screen gestures or the navigation buttons to navigate your phone.

Button		Function
III	Recents	• Tap to open the list of recent apps.
O	Home	• Tap to return to the Home screen. • Tap and hold to launch the **Google Assistant** app.
<	Back	• Tap to return to the previous screen.

Navigation buttons

For fast navigation, make use of the buttons located at the screen's bottom.

1. Navigate to Settings >  Display > Navigation bar > Buttons.

2. Under Button order, select the location that you want the Recent apps icons and the Back icon to be displayed.

Navigation gestures

For your screen not to be obstructed, hide the buttons for navigation at the screen's bottom. Then swipe for device navigation.

1. To enable the Swipe gestures feature, navigate to Settings > Display > Navigation bar > Swipe gestures.

2. Tap any of the option to customize:

• More options: Select the type and sensitivity of a gesture.

• Gesture hints: This displays lines at the screen's bottom where the screen gestures are located.

• Show button to hide keyboard: Anytime the device is in portrait, this feature shows an icon at the screen's bottom right corner to hide the keyboard.

- Block gestures with S Pen: This feature stops the S Pen from making navigation gestures (available only in the Galaxy S21 Ultra 5G).

Chapter 4: Home Screen Customization

Your device's navigation start point is the Home screen. Here, you can place the widgets and apps that you like. Other activities that you can perform here include changing the screen order, setting up and removing more home screens, and selecting your main home screen.

App icons

Make use of an app's icon to launch the app from any location on the Home screen.

- Navigate to Apps, then hold down the icon of the app and tap ⊕ Add to Home. For icon removal:
- From the Home screen, hold down the

icon of an app, then tap 🗑 Remove.

💡 Note that when you remove an icon, the app will not be deleted, just the icon will be removed from the home screen.

Wallpaper

Select your preferred image, video, or wallpaper to change how your Lock and the Home screen looks.

1. Hold down any part of the Home screen then tap 🖼 Wallpapers.

2. Select any of the menus below to view the wallpapers available:

• My wallpapers: Select one from your downloaded or featured wallpapers.

• Gallery: Select videos and images from the Gallery app.

• Wallpaper services: Activate more

features like the Dynamic lock screen and Guide page.

- Apply Dark mode to Wallpaper: Activate this to apply Dark mode on your wallpaper.
- Explore more wallpapers: Locate and download other wallpapers from Galaxy Themes.

3. Tap a video or picture to select it.

- If you are choosing a single picture, select the screen or screens that you want the wallpaper to be applied to.
- You can apple different videos and pictures only to the lock screen.
- When choosing videos and pictures from the Gallery, and then tap any of the items and tap done.

4. Tap either set on lock and Home

Screens, depending on the screen you use. Set on Lock and Home screens or Set on Home screen.

If you want to apply wallpaper to the Home and Lock Screens, then have the Sync my edits feature activated to affect any edits done on the wallpaper so you can apply it to both screens.

Themes

You can set set a theme for your app icons, Home and Lock screen and wallpapers;

1. Have any part of the Hold down any part of the Home screen.

2. Tap Themes, then tap a theme to preview and download it.

3. Tap Navigation drawer > My stuff

> Themes to see downloaded themes.

4. Tap a theme, and tap Apply to apply it.

Icons

Apply any icon set as a replacement for the default icons.

1. Hold down any part of the home screen.

2. Tap Themes > Icons, then tap an icon set to preview and download it.

3. Tap Navigation drawer > My stuff > Icons to view the icons downloaded.

4. To apply an icon set, tap an icon, then tap Apply.

Widgets

To get fast access to apps and info, add

widgets to your home screens.

1. Hold down any part of the Home screen.

2. Tap ⋮⋮ Widgets, and then open a widget set by tapping any of it.

3. Tap add after swiping to the widget that you want to add to your Home screen.

Customize Widgets

You can customize the location and function of any widget that you have added.

○ Hold down a Widget located in a Home screen and tap on any of the following options:

- 🗑 Remove: Delete a widget from your screen.
- ⚙ Settings: Customize the

widget's appearance or function.

- ⓘ App info: Review the widget's permissions, usage, and more.

Home screen settings

Customize your Apps and Home screens.

1. Hold down any location on the home screen.

2. Tap ⚙ Settings to customize:

- Home screen layout: Setup your phone to feature different Apps and Home screens or just a Home screen where the apps will be located.
- Home screen grid: Select a layout to determine the arrangement of the icons on the Home screen.
- Apps screen grid: Choose a layout to determine how icons are arranged on the Apps screen.

- Show Apps screen button on Home screen: Add a Home screen button to get easy access to the Apps screen.
- Lock Home screen layout: This feature prevents the Home screen's items from being repositioned or removed.
- Add new apps to the Home screen: Add new apps that can be downloaded to the Home screen.
- Hide apps: Select the apps to hide from the Apps and Home screens. To restore hidden apps, return to this screen.

The hidden apps are still installed and can be displayed as results in searches.

- App icon badges: Enable this to show badges on apps that have active notifications. You can also select the style of the badge.

- Swipe down for the notification panel: Swipe down anywhere on the Home screen to enter the Notification panel.
- Rotate to landscape mode: This feature automatically rotates the Home screen when the orientation of your device has been changed.
- About Home screen: View info concerning the version.

Easy mode

There are larger icons and text in the Easy mode layout. This enables an easier viewing experience. Simply switch between a simpler layout and the default screen layout.

1. Navigate to Settings > Display > Easy mode.

2. Tap ● to activate this feature. When you do this, the following options will appear:

• Touch and hold delay: Set the duration for a continuous touch to be processed as touch and hold.

• High contrast keyboard: Select a keyboard having high contrast colors.

Status bar

In the Status bar, the notification alerts are on the left while information concerning the device is on the right side.

Status icons

Battery full   Charging   Mute   Vibrate

Airplane mode   Bluetooth active
   Location active

Alarm

Notification icons

Missed calls Call in progress   New messageVoicemail

New email   Download   Upload   App update

Set up the Status bar's display options.

○ Go to Quick Settings, tap ⋮ More options > Status bar to get the following options:

• Show notification icons: Select how the information will be displayed on the Status bar.
• Show battery percentage: Show the percentage of the battery next to the battery's icon on the status bar.

Chapter 5: Notification panel

Open the Notification panel for quick access to Settings, Notifications, and more.

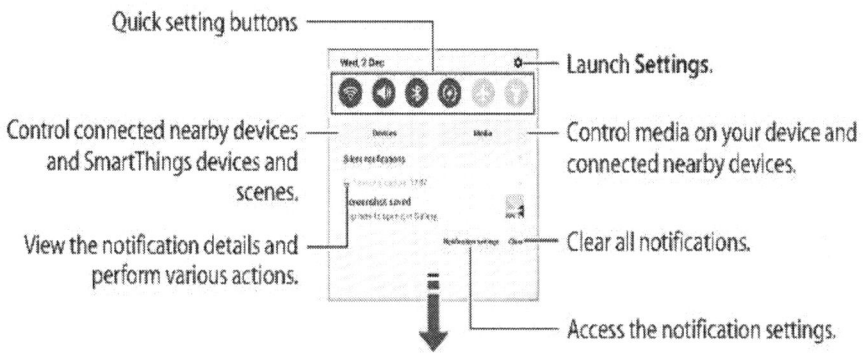

View the Notification panel

Via any screen, you can enter the Notification panel.

1. Swipe the screen down to show the Notification panel.
- Tap an item to open it.
- Drag a notification right or left to clear it.
- Tap Clear to clear all the notifications.
- Tap the Notification settings to customize the notifications.

2. To close back the notification panel, drag the screen upwards from its bottom.

Alternatively, tap Back to close the Notification panel.

Quick settings

Via the Notification panel, you can quickly access the different functions of the device using Quick settings.

See Quick Settings by swiping down from the screen's top with two fingers f.

- Tap Finder search to search the device.

- Tap Power ff for Power off, Emergency mode, and Restart options.
- Tap Open settings to enter the settings menu of the device fast.
- Tap More options to change the layout of the Quick settings button or just

reorder the Quick settings.

- After installing supported apps like Google Home, SmartThings, you can enter Devices to control them.
- Tap Media to enter the Media panel and control video devices and connected audio.
- Tap the icon of a quick setting to turn it off or on.
- Open the setting of a Quick Setting by holding down its icon.
- Adjust the brightness of the screen by adjusting the Brightness slider.

Air view

You can preview info concerning an item on the screen by hovering the S Pen over the screen. The following Air view features are present:

- Preview a mail before you open it.
- Preview a photo album or perform a picture enlargement.
- Hover over the timeline of a video to preview the video and also skip to a particular scene.
- See the description and name of a button or icon.

💡 Note that the preview function is only present when the color of the S Pen's pointer is solid.

Screen off memo

You do not have to turn on the screen to write memos.

1. Press the button on the S Pen when the screen is off, then tap the screen.
2. To customize your memo, tap any of the options below:

- ◯ Color: Change the pen color.
- ✏ Pen settings: Tap to make use of the pen tool. Double-tap to adjust the thickness of the line.
- 🧽 Eraser: Tap to make use of the eraser tool. Double-tap to erase it all.

3. Save your meme to the Samsung Notes app by tapping Save.

💡 Note that you have to enable the screen off memo settings.

Pin to Always On Display

You can either edit or pin a memo on the Always On Display.

1. Go to the screen off memo, and tap 📌 Pin to Always on Display.
2. Tap Pin to Always On Display.

AR Doodle

Using augmented reality, you can draw interactive doodles on object or faces that are seen through your device camera or other objects seen through the camera.

1. Tap Air command > AR Doodle.
2. Select either rear or front cameras by tapping Switch cameras.
3. Place the camera in a way that the target will be in the screen's center.
4. Draw a doodle using the S Pen.
• In real-time, the doodle follows the face movement.
5. Tap Rec

Parental controls and Digital wellbeing

You can manage and monitor your online life by getting a daily listing of your most frequently used apps. Also know the number of notifications that you receive and the frequency with which you use your phone. Also, you can configure your phone to enable rest well before you sleep.

○ To get the following features, navigate to Settings, then tap ◎ Digital Wellbeing and parental controls:

• To see the following, tap the Dashboard:

- Screen time: See the time duration of which an app has been opened and use every day.

- Notifications received: See the daily number of notifications received by an app.
- Unlocks: See the number of times an app has been accessed every day.

Your goals

- Screen time: Set up a goal for your screen time and see your average each day.
- App timers: Set the limit for the daily usage of each app.

Ways to disconnect

- Focus mode: Set a limit for how you use your apps for a certain time so as not to distract you.

- Bedtime mode: Configure the time that your screen should switch to grayscale and also mute alerts, sounds, and calls.

Comfort care

- Volume monitor: Select a source of sound to safeguard your ears as well as monitor the volume.

Check on your kids

- Parental controls: Use Google's Family Link app to monitor how your kids make use of the device. You can set content filters, select apps, and monitor and set limits for screen time.

Always On Display

Make use of the Always On Display(AOD) to see message alerts, check the date and time, see missed calls and other customized info without unlocking your phone.

1. Navigate to Settings > 🔒 Lock screen > Always On Display.

2. Tap ⬤ to activate the feature, and also see the following options:

• Select the duration of which you notifications and the clock will be shown on the screen anytime you are not making use of the device. Tap any of the following: 10 seconds, Show as scheduled, or Show always.

• Clock style: Change the color option and clock style on the Always on Display and Lock screen.

• Show music information: This

displays the details of the music being played anytime the controller of the FaceWidgets music is in use.

- Screen orientation: View the AOD in either landscape or portrait mode.
- Auto brightness: Adjust the Always On Display brightness automatically.
- About Always On Display: See the license info and currents version of the software.

💡 Note that certain display settings can be displayed on both the Always on Display and the Lock screen. To learn more visit Clock and information.

AOD themes

Apply custom themes for the Always On Display.

1. Hold down any part of the Home

screen and tap Themes > AODs.

- Tap an AOD to preview it. Then download it to My Always On Displays.

2. Tap Navigation drawer > My stuff > AODs to view your downloaded themes.

3. Tap any AOD, then tap Apply.

Chapter 6: Enter text

You can enter a text using your voice or a keyboard.

Toolbar

You can quickly access the keyboard's features on the toolbar, though the options may differ depending on the carrier.

- Go to Samsung keyboard and This gives an expanded toolbar having the following options:

- ☺ Emojis: Insert an emoji.
- 🗒 Stickers: Add illustrated stickers.
- GIFs: Add animated GIFs.
- 🎤 Voice input: Make use of Samsung voice input.
- ⚙ Settings: Access the settings of the keyboard.
- ✎ Handwriting: Make use of your handwriting to input texts (for Galaxy S21 Ultra 5G only).
- 🔍 Search: Search for specific phrases and words in your conversations.
- 🌐 Translate: Input sentences or words into the keyboard to translate them to a different language.
- Samsung Pass: Utilize biometrics

to secure your services and apps.

- Spotify: Add music from Spotify™.
- YouTube: Add videos from YouTube.
- Clipboard: Access the clipboard.
- Text editing: Make use of an editing panel to pinpoint the texts that you want to copy, cut, and paste.
- Modes: Choose the layout for your keyboard.
- Keyboard size: Adjust your keyboard's width and height.
- Bitmoji: Make your own emoji and use it as stickers.
- AR Emoji: Make your own emoji and use them as shareable stickers.
- Mojitok: Make your stickers or insert the suggested ones automatically.

Samsung Keyboard Configuration

Configure your Samsung keyboard.

○ To get the following options, go to the Samsung keyboard and tap ⚙ Settings:

• Languages and types: Select the type of keyboard and choose the languages that you want on the keyboard.

− Swipe the Space bar either right or left to switch between languages.

Smart typing

• Predictive text: This gives you suggested phrases and words as you type.

- Suggest emojis: This adds emojis when you are using predictive text.
- Suggest stickers while typing: View the recommended stickers when typing.
- Auto replace: Automatically replace what you are typing with the predictive text recommendations.
- Auto spell check: This feature underlines words that are misspelled in red, then suggest corrections.
- More typing options: Customize the additional typing options.

Style and layout

- Keyboard toolbar: Hide or unhide the keyboard's toolbar.
- High contrast keyboard: Adjust the

Samsung keyboard's size and also change its colors to increase the contrast between the background and the keys.

- Theme: Select a keyboard theme.
- Mode: Select either landscape or portrait mode.
- Size and transparency: Adjust the keyboard's transparency and size.
- Layout: Show special characters and numbers on the keyboard.
- Font size: Adjust the size of the font by dragging the slider.
- Custom symbols: Change the shortcuts for the keyboard's symbols.

Other settings

- Touch, swipe, and feedback: Customize the feedback and gestures.
- Handwriting: Customize the

handwriting options (for Galaxy S21 Ultra 5G only).

- Choose third-party content to use: Enable the keyboard's third-party features.
- Reset to default settings: Take the keyboard back to its default settings and clear the personalized data.
- About Samsung keyboard: View the Samsung Keyboard's legal information and software version.

- Contact us: Make use of Samsung Members to contact the Samsung support (if it is supported by your carrier).

Use Samsung voice input

Input text by speaking instead of typing.

○ Go to the Samsung keyboard, and tap ◍ Voice input, then speak your text.

Configure the Samsung voice input

Set your customized options for the Samsung voice input.

1. Go to the Samsung keyboard, and tap ◍ Voice input.

2. To get the following options, Tap ⚙ Settings.

• Keyboard language: Select your keyboard's language.

• Voice input language: Choose the language for the Samsung voice input.

• Hide offensive words: Use asterisks to hide words that may be offensive.

• About Samsung voice input: See the

legal information and software version for the Samsung voice input.

Emergency mode

Make use of the Emergency mode to get access to important emergency features and also save your phone's battery during an emergency.

For battery power saving, Emergency mode:

- Restricts the usage of apps to only important apps and those you have chosen.
- Switches off the mobile data and connectivity features anytime the screen is off.

Activate Emergency mode

To activate the Emergency mode:

1. Simultaneously press and hold the Volume Down and Side buttons.
2. Tap ⬤ Emergency mode.
- Upon first access, read and accept the terms and conditions.
3. Tap Turn on.

Emergency mode features

In Emergency Mode, only the apps listed below are available on the Home screen. The options may differ by carrier.

- Estimated battery life: This displays the estimated battery time remaining depending on the battery usage and charge.
- Flashlight: Make use of the phone's

flash as a steady light source.

● Emergency alarm: Sound a loud siren.

● Phone: Open the call screen.

● Message/Share my location: Send info concerning your location to emergency contacts.

● Internet: Access the internet.

● Chrome: Open the Google web browser.

● Emergency call: Dial an emergency phone number (example, 911). You can make this type of call without an activated service.

● ⋮ More options:

− Turn off Emergency mode: Deactivate Emergency mode and reverse to standard mode.

− Edit: Add or take away apps from the

screen.

- Emergency contacts: Manage your ICE(In Case of Emergency) contacts and medical profile.

- Settings: Set up the available settings. Just a few settings are available in Emergency mode.

Deactivate Emergency mode

When the emergency mode is deactivated, the device will return to standard mode.

○ Tap ⋮

Biometric security

Utilize the biometrics to log into your accounts and also secure your device.

Face recognition

You can make use of Face Recognition to unlock your phone. To do this, you have to also set either a password, PIN, or pattern.

- Password, Pin, and Pattern are more secure than Face recognition. While using Face recognition, someone who looks like you can unlock your phone.
- Certain circumstances can affect face recognition. These include beards, wearing hats, glasses, or heavy makeup.

- Be sure that you are in a place that is well lit when you are registering your face. Also, make sure that the lens of the camera is neat.

1. Navigate to Settings > ⚙ Biometrics and security > Face recognition.

2. To register your face, carry out the displayed instructions.

Face recognition management

Configure the workability of the face recognition.

◦ Navigate to Settings > ◯ Biometrics and security > Face recognition.

• Remove face data: Erase the existing faces.

• Add alternative look: Include another appearance to enhance the face recognition.

• Face unlock: Disable or enable the security of the face recognition.

• Stay on Lock screen until swipe: Anytime that you utilize the Face recognition to unlock your device, your phone will still be on the Lock screen till you perform a screen swipe.

- Faster recognition: Enable this feature for faster face recognition. Disable it to increase the security, thereby making it more difficult for your device to be unlocked with a video or picture that looks like you.
- Require open eyes: Only with eyes open will the facial recognition system recognize your face.
- Brighten screen: Temporarily increase the brightness of the screen to enable your face to be recognized in dark environments.
- About unlocking with biometrics: Know more about using biometrics to secure your device.

Fingerprint scanner

Make use of fingerprint recognition instead of passwords for certain applications.

Also, you can utilize your fingerprint for identity verification for your Samsung Account login. To make use of the fingerprint, you have to set up either a password, PIN, or Pattern.

1. Navigate to Settings > ⚙ Biometrics and security > Fingerprints.

2. Carry put the displayed instructions for your fingerprint registration.

Fingerprint management

Rename, delete and add new fingerprints.

○ To get the following options, navigate to Settings > ⚙ Biometrics and security > Fingerprints:

- A list having the registered fingerprints are located at this list's beginning. Tap any fingerprint other to rename or delete it.
- Add fingerprint: To register a new fingerprint, carry out the instructions as displayed.
- Check added fingerprints: To know if your fingerprint has been registered, simply scan the fingerprints.

Fingerprint verification settings

Utilize fingerprint recognition for identity verification in compatible apps.

- Navigate to Settings > Biometrics and security > Fingerprints.
- Fingerprint unlock: Make use of your fingerprint to identify yourself when you are unlocking the device.

• Fingerprint always on: You can scan your fingerprint even when the display is not on.

• Show icon when screen is off: This displays the icon of the fingerprint even when the screen is not on.

• Show animation when unlocking: This displays an animation when you are making use of the fingerprint verification.

• About unlocking with biometrics: Learn more about the requirements needed for using the password, PIN or pattern as a backup.

Biometrics settings

Set up your biometric security options preferences.

◦ To view the following, navigate to Settings > Biometrics and security >

More biometrics settings:

• Show unlock transition effect: This displays a transition effect anytime you unlock your device using biometrics.

• Biometrics security patch: See the version of the software that the biometric security uses.

Mobile continuity

Gain access to different device functions and storage features from other compatible computers and gadgets.

Link to Windows | Samsung DeX | Continue apps on other devices

Link to Windows

Achieve continuity between Windows-based computers and your device. Gain quick access to your messages, images, and other items by linking your device to a compatible PC.

Pictures

• Drag and drop pictures in Windows.

• Gain access to the images and edit them in the Photos app.

• Use Windows to share the pictures with your contacts.

Messages (SMS/MMS)

• Supports MMS group messaging.

• Integration with Windows Emoji Picker.

• Get a Windows pop-up anytime a new message is received.

Chapter 7: Using Apps

All the downloaded or preloaded apps are displayed in the Apps list. You can download apps from the Google Play™ store and Galaxy Store

◌ To view the Apps list, swipe up the screen from the Home screen.

Disable or Uninstall apps

You can remove the apps that you installed while apps that came preloaded can only be disabled. The disabled apps are switched off and hidden from the Apps list.

◌ Go to Apps, and hold an app, then tap Uninstall/Disable.

Search for apps

You can make use of the Search feature if you don't know where to locate a setting or app.

1. Go to Apps and tap Search, then input the words or word. When you type, corresponding settings and apps will be displayed on the screen.
2. Tap a result access it.

To customize the search settings just navigate to More options > Settings.

Sort apps

You can list shortcuts in alphabetical order or your custom order.

○ Go to Apps, tap More options > Sort

to get the following sorting options:

- Custom order: Manually arrange apps.
- Alphabetical order: Sort apps alphabetically.

💡 Note that apps can be arranged manually or in a custom order. You can remove empty icon spaces via ⋮ More options > Clean up pages.

Create and use folders

On the Apps list, you can make the folders to organize the shortcuts for the Apps.

1. Go to Apps, press and hold the shortcut of an app and drag it to the top of another app shortcut till it is

highlighted.

2. Create a folder by releasing the shortcut of the app.

- Folder name: Name the folder.
- ○ Palette: Change the color of the folder.
- ＋ Add apps: Put more apps in the folder. Tap an app to select it then tap Done.

3. Tap ＜ Back to exit the folder.

Copy a folder to a Home screen

You can copy a folder to a location on the Home screen.

○ Go to Apps, press and hold a folder, then tap ⊕ Add to Home.

Delete a folder

The app shortcuts of a deleted folder will return to the Apps list.

1. Go to Apps, press and hold a folder to delete it.

2. Tap Delete folder, then confirm when asked to.

Game Booster

Based on game usage, you can get optimized performance for your gameplay. Enable features such as Dolby Atmos, or Bixby and block notifications and calls.

 Swipe up from the screen's bottom when playing a game to see the navigation bar. You can see the following options on the far left and right sides:

- Screen touch lock: Prevent accidental taps by locking the screen. This option comes default.
- Game Booster: Setup other options such as screen touches, performance monitoring, screenshots, and navigation bar blocking.

App settings

Manage your preloaded and downloaded apps.

○ Navigate to Settings > Apps. Tap any option to customize:

- Select default apps: Select the apps for sending messages, making calls, surfing the web, and more.

• Samsung app settings: View your Samsung apps list and customize their settings.

• Your apps: Tap an app to see and update its usage and privacy settings information. The options differ by app.

💡 To reset app options that have been changed, go to ⋮ More options > Reset app preferences.

Microsoft apps

The Microsoft apps below may come preloaded on your device. Also, the apps can be downloaded from the Google Play Store and the Galaxy Store.

Outlook

Get access to tasks, contacts, calendars, and more via Outlook.

LinkedIn

Connect with other world professionals of different fields.

Office

Make use of the Microsoft Office app to enjoy the PowerPoint, Excel and Word apps on your mobile device.

OneDrive

Save and share documents, videos, photos, and more in your free online OneDrive® account. You can access them from your phone, tablet, or PC.

Samsung Apps

The following apps can be downloaded to your device or may come preloaded be preloaded. You can download apps from the Google Play™ store or the Galaxy Store.

Galaxy Essentials

Galaxy Essentials is an assemblage of apps that are specially chosen via the Samsung apps. You can get and download the premium content.

- Go to Apps > ⋮ More options > Galaxy Essentials.

 AR Zone

Get access to all the Augmented Reality (AR) features. To know more, see AR Zone.

Bixby

Bixby displays content that is customized based on your interaction. Bixby learns how you use your device and suggests content that may please you.

Galaxy Shop

This is the best means to shop for Samsung products, stay updated on the next Galaxy device and unlock premium offers.

**Galaxy Store**

Locate and download Galaxy device exclusive premium apps. To download from the Galaxy Store, a Samsung account is needed.

Galaxy Wearable

Use this app to link your device to your Samsung Watch.

Game Launcher

Arrange all your games automatically in one location. Go to Settings > ⚙ Advanced features > Game launcher, tap ⬤ if you cant find the Game Launcher on the Apps list.

PENUP

Comment on photos, create your own or browse through the collections to get what to include in your own collection. This community brings together users of the S Pen for painting, scribbling, sketching or drawing.

Samsung Free

For free, you can access live news, articles, and TV shows from different sources.

Samsung Global Goals

From this app, you can know more about the Global Goals initiative and contribute towards these causes via ads.

Samsung Members

Access more and do more with your Galaxy device. Enjoy exclusive content and DIY support tools, only for Samsung members. The Samsung Members may come preloaded on your device or you can download and install it from the Google Play Store or Galaxy Store.

Samsung TV Plus

Enjoy entertainment, news, and more for free on your Samsung mobile and TV devices.

SmartThings

SmartThings lets you automate, monitor and control your home area via your mobile device as you desire. You can make use of the app to connect to one or more devices simultaneously.

Simply look at the dashboard to check the devices' statuses.

💡 Note that the errors related to the connected devices which are non Samsung are not Samsung warranty-covered. For support, contact the device manufacturer.

Tips

See users manual, techniques and tips for your device.

Calculator

The Calculator app has both scientific and basic math functions. It also has unit converter.

Calendar

You can connect the Calendar app to your online accounts to keep your calendars together.

Add calendars

Add your accounts to the Calendar app.

1. Go to Calendar, tap Navigation drawer.

2. Tap Calendar settings > Add account and choose an account type.

3. Input your account info and follow the prompts.

The accounts may support contacts, email, and other features.

Subscription calendars

Subscribe to calendars that interests you. You can see different upcoming events and include them in your schedule.

1. Go to 🅞 Calendar, tap ☰ Navigation drawer.
2. Tap Add your interests and obey the prompts.

Calendar alert style

You can set the Calendar Alerts to different styles.

1. Go to 🅞 Calendar, tap ☰ Navigation drawer > ⚙ Calendar settings > Alert style. You will see the following options:
- Light: Get a notification and listen to a short sound.
- Medium: Receive a full-screen alert

and listen to a short sound.

- Strong: Receive a full-screen alert and ring tone that won't stop till it is dismissed.

2. The following sound options are present based on the chosen alert style:

- Ring once sound: Select the alert sound for Medium or Light alert styles.

- Keep ringing sound: Select the alert sound for the Strong alert style.

Create an event

Create events with your Calendar.

1. To add an event, navigate to Calendar, and tap Add event.

2. Enter the event details and tap Save.

Delete an event

Erase your Calendar events.

1. To edit an event, go to Calendar, tap the event twice.

2. Tap Delete, and follow the prompt to confirm.

Clock

The Clock app has time tracking and alarm setting features.

Alarm

Make use of the Alarm tab to set s recurring or one-time alarm. Also select notification options.

1. Go to Clock, tap Add alarm.

2. To configure an alarm, tap the following items:

- Time: Set an alarm time.
- Day: Select an alarm day or days.

- Alarm name: Enter an alarm name.
- Alarm sound: Select an alarm sound and volume.
- Vibration: Select whether the alarm should vibrate.
- Snooze: Enable snoozing. Set repeat values and time intervals for the alarm when snoozing.

3. Tap Save to store the alarm.

Delete an alarm

You can erase an alarm that you made.

1. Go to Clock, then press and hold an alarm.
2. Tap Delete.

Alert settings

Whenever the Sound mode is set to

Vibrate or Mute, you can still set the timer alarm to vibrate.

1. Go to Clock, tap More options > Settings.

2. To activate, tap Vibrate for alarms and timers.

World clock

The World clock allows you know current time of different cities in the world.

1. Go to Clock, tap World clock.

2. Tap Add city.

3. Press and hold the globe to spin it, then tap your city of choice and tap Add.

• Press and hold any city that you want to remove, then tap Delete.

Time zone converter

Select a city's time to see the time for other listed cities.

1. Go to 🕐 Clock > World clock.
2. Tap ⋮ More options > Time zone converter.
3. Tap ▼ Menu to select a different city.

- To include another city, tap ➕ Add city.

4. To set a time, swipe the minute, hours, and period (PM or AM) on the clock. The local times for other listed cities are updated automatically.

- Tap Reset to take the clock back to the current time.

Weather settings

Display weather information on the World

clock.

1. Navigate to ⊙ Clock > World clock.

2. Tap ⋮ More options > Settings > Show weather information to disable or enable the weather information.

3. Tap Unit to switch from Fahrenheit to Celsius.

Stopwatch

The Stopwatch allows you to time down events up to a hundredth of a second.

1. Navigate to ⊙ Clock > Stopwatch.

2. To start timing, Tap Start.

• Tap Lap to keep track of lap times.

3. Tap Stop to stop timing.

• Tap Resume to continue the timing even after the clock is stopped.

• Tap Reset to reset the Stopwatch to zero.

Timer

Set up a timer for countdown up to 99 hours, 59 minutes, and 59 seconds.

1. Go to ◉ Clock > Timer.
2. Using the keypad, input the Seconds, Minutes, and Hours of the Timer.
3. To start the Timer, tap Start.

- To stop the timer temporarily, tap Pause. Tap Resume to continue.
- Tap Cancel to stop and reset the Timer.

Preset timer

Name and store preset timers.

1. Go to ◉ Clock > Timer > + Add a preset timer.
2. Set up the timer name and the countdown time.

3. To save the timer Tap Add.

- To edit a saved preset timer, tap More options > Edit preset timers.

Timer options

You can configure the Timer options to your taste.

1. Navigate to ⊙ Clock > Timer.
2. Tap More options > Settings.

- Sound: Select a preloaded timer sound or put your own.

- Vibration: Disable or enable the timer vibration.

General settings

See and configure all your Clock tools settings.

○ Go to ⊙ Clock, tap ⋮ More options >

Settings.

- Customization Service: To customize the different supported apps personalized contents, sign in to your Samsung account.
- About Clock: See the current software version and check for updates.

Chapter 8: Contacts

Save and manage your contacts. You can synchronize them with your accounts. The Accounts may also support email, calendars, and other features.

Create a contact

1. Go to Contacts, tap Create contact.

2. Input the contact details, and tap Save.

Edit a contact

During the editing of contact, you can delete or change the info of a field. Also, you can extra fields to the contact info.

1. Go to Contacts, and tap a contact.

2. Tap Edit.

3. Tap on any field to change, add or

delete the info.

4. Tap Save.

Favorites

When you tag a contact as favorites, they are grouped at top of your contact list and can be easily accessed from other apps.

1. Go to Contacts, and tap a contact.

2. Tap ☆ Favorites to tag the contact as a favorite.

• Tap ★ Favorites if you want to remove the contact from Favorites

Share a contact

Use different sharing services and methods to share a contact with others.

1. Go to Contacts and tap a contact.

2. Tap Share.

3. Tap either Text or File.

4. Select a method for sharing then follow the displayed prompts.

When you are viewing a contact, tap ⋮ More options > QR code to quickly share the information with family and friends.

The QR code automatically updates when you edit the fields of the contact information.

Display contacts when sharing content

You can directly share content with your contact using any app. When you enable this feature, the contacts that you access frequently will be shown in the Share window.

○ Go to Settings > ⚙ Advanced features > Show contacts when sharing content.

Then tap ● to enable the feature.

Groups

You can organize your contacts using groups.

Create a group

Create your contact groups.

1. Go to ● Contacts, tap ≡ Open drawer > Groups.

2. Tap Create group, then tap fields to input the group information:

• Group name: Input the group name.

• Group ringtone: Customize the group sounds.

• Add member: Choose the contacts to add to the new group, then tap Done.

3. Tap Save.

Add or remove group contacts

Add or remove contacts from the group.

○ Go to Contacts, tap Open drawer > Groups, then tap a group.

- To delete a contact, press and hold the contact to select it, then tap Remove.
- To add a contact, tap Edit > Add member, then tap the contacts that you want to add. When you are finished, tap Done > Save.

Send a message to a group

Send the group members a text message.

1. Go to Contacts, tap Open drawer > Groups, then tap a group.

2. Tap More options > Send message.

Send an email to a group

Send your group members an email.

1. Go to 👤 Contacts, tap ☰ Open drawer > Groups, then tap a group.
2. Tap ⋮ More options > Send email.
3. Select a contact by tapping it. Alternatively, tap the All checkbox located at the screen's top to select all, then tap Done.

• Only the group members having their email addresses recorded will be displayed.

4. Select an email account, then follow the displayed prompts.

Delete a group

Delete a group that you have created.

1. Go to ⊖ Contacts, tap ≡ Open drawer > Groups, then tap a group.
2. Tap ⋮ More options > Delete.
- Tap Group only to delete the group.
- Tap Group and members to delete the group and its contacts.

Manage contacts

You can export and import contacts. Also, you can consolidate different contacts as one contact entry.

Merge contacts

Unify the information of different contacts into one contact by linking their entries as one contact.

1. Go to 👤 Contacts, tap ≡ Open drawer > Manage contacts.

2. Tap Merge contacts. The contacts having duplicate names, phone numbers, and email addresses will be grouped.

3. Select the contacts by tapping them, then tap Merge.

Delete duplicate contacts

Remove duplicated contacts fast.

1. Go to 👤 Contacts, tap ≡ Open drawer > Manage contacts.

2. Tap Delete duplicate contacts. The contacts that are duplicated will be listed.

3. Select the contacts by tapping on them, then tap Delete.

Import contacts

Import contacts to your device in the form of vCard files (VCF).

1. Go to Contacts, tap Open drawer > Manage contacts.
2. Tap Import or export contacts.
3. Tap Import, then follow the prompts.

Export contacts

Export contacts from your device in the form of vCard files (VCF).

1. Go to Contacts tap Open drawer > Manage contacts.
2. Tap Import or export contacts.
3. Tap Export then follow the prompts.

Sync contacts

Maintain an updated contact list in all

your accounts.

1. Go to 👤 Contacts tap ≡ Open drawer > Manage contacts.

2. Tap Sync contacts.

Set the default storage location

Save the new contacts automatically to your SIM card, account, or device.

1. Go to 👤 Contacts, tap ≡ Open drawer > Manage contacts.

2. Tap on Set default storage location.

3. Add an account or tap any of the options to set the default.

Delete contacts

Delete a single or multiple contacts.

1. Go to 👤 Contacts. Select any contact by holding it.
- If you want to delete any contact,

tap it to select.

2. Tap  Delete, and follow the prompt.

Internet

The Samsung Internet is a quick, simple, and reliable mobile web browser. Experience a secured Web browsing experience with different features such as Contents Blocker, Secret Mode, and Biometric Web Login.

Browser tabs

Make use of the tabs to see different web pages together.

○ Go to Internet > Tabs > New tab.

- To exit a tab, tap Tabs > Close

tab.

Create a Bookmark

Quickly access your favorite webpages by bookmarking them.

- To save an open webpage, go to Internet > ☆ Bookmark.

Open a Bookmark

Launch a Bookmarked page quickly.

1. Navigate to Internet > ☆ Bookmarks.
2. Tap a bookmark entry.

Save a web page

In the Samsung Internet app, there are different options for saving a webpage.

- Go to Internet, tap Tools > Add

page to get the following options:

- Bookmarks: Include the webpage in your Bookmark list.
- Quick access: See a list of saved web pages or the ones you access regularly.
- Home screen: Create a webpage shortcut on your Home screen.
- Saved pages: Save the content of the webpage to your device to enable you to view it offline.

View history

To see a list of web pages you visited recently:

○ Go to Internet, tap ≡ Tools > History.

💡To erase your browsing history, navigate to ⋮ More options >

Clear history.

Share pages

You can share web pages with your contacts.

○ Go to Internet, tap ≡ Tools > Share, and follow the displayed prompts.

Secret mode

The pages that you view in secret mode will not be listed in your search or browser history, leaving no trace or cookies on your device. The secret tabs are a shade darker than the normal tabs.

After you close a secret tab, the files you

downloaded will remain on your device.

1. Go to 🔍 Internet > 🗔 Tabs > Turn on secret mode.

2. To start the secret mode browsing, tap Start.

Secret mode settings

This feature requires a biometric lock or password to make use of the secret mode.

1. Go to 🔍 Internet, tap 🗔 Tabs.

2. Tap ⋮ More options > Secret mode settings to get the following options:

• Use password: use a password to enable secret mode.

• Face: Make use of Face recognition to keep the Secret mode private.

• Fingerprints: Make use of a

Fingerprint scanner to keep the Secret mode private.

- Reset Secret mode: Erase the data of your secret mode and restore it to default.

Turn off secret mode

This disables secret mode and returns you to normal browsing.

○ Go to ● Internet > ▫ Tabs > Turn off secret mode.

Internet settings

Modify the settings linked with making use of the Internet app.

○ Go to ● Internet, tap ≡ Tools > Settings.

Chapter 9: Phone

Apart from making telephone calls, the Phone apps perform other actions. Make use of the advanced calling features. To know more, contact your carrier for more information. The appearance of the Phone app screen differs based on the carrier.

Calls

The Phone app lets you receive and make calls via the Recents tab, Contact, Home screen, and others.

Make a call

Make use of your phone to answer and make calls via the Home screen.

○ Navigate to Phone, input a number on the keypad, and tap Call.

- Tap the Keypad if it is not displayed.

Make a call from Recents

All the missed, outgoing, and incoming calls are recorded in the Call log.

1. Navigate to Phone > Recents to see the list of recent calls.

2. Tap a contact, then tap Call.

Make a call from Contacts

Call a contact via the Contacts app.

○ Navigate to Contacts, and swipe your finger to the right across a contact to call the contact.

Answer a call

When you receive a call, the phone will ring with the caller's name and phone number displayed. If you are making use of an app, a pop-up screen will display the incoming call.

- On the screen for incoming call screen, drag the ⓒ Answer icon to the right to answer it.

💡 On the pop-up screen for the incoming call, tap 📞 Answer to receive it.

Decline a call

You can decide to decline an incoming call. If you are making use of an app, a pop-up screen for the incoming call will be displayed.

- Drag ⌒ Decline to the left of the incoming call screen to reject the call and redirect it to your voicemail.

💡 On the pop-up screen for incoming call, tap ⌒ Decline to reject the call and redirect it to your voicemail.

Decline with a message

You can decide to decline an incoming call using a text message response.

- On the screen for the incoming call, drag the Send message menu upward, and choose a message.

💡 On the pop-up screen for the incoming call, tap Send message and choose a message.

End a call

- Tap End call when you want to end the call.

Actions while on a call

While on a call, you can switch to a speaker or headset, adjust the volume of the call volume, and even multitask.

○ To decrease or increase the volume, press the Volume keys to increase.

Switch to speaker or headset

Listen to a call using a Bluetooth® headset (not included) or a speaker.

○ Tap 🔊 Speaker to listen to the caller using the speaker or tap Bluetooth to listen to the caller using a Bluetooth headset.

Multitask

If you go out of the call screen to make use of another app, your call which is still active will be displayed in the Status bar.

To go back to the call screen:

○ Tap the call after dragging down the Status bar down to show the Notification panel.

To end a call while multitasking:

○ Drag down the Status bar to show the Notification panel, then tap End call.

Call background

Choose a picture or video to be displayed anytime you receive or make a call.

○ Go to Phone, tap More options > Settings > Call background to see the following options:

- Layout: Choose the way the caller's

info will be displayed if there is a profile picture for the person.

• Background: Select a picture to be displayed during a call.

Call pop-up settings

A call can be displayed as pop-ups when they are received while making use of other apps.

○ Go to Phone, tap ⋮ More options > Settings > Call display while using apps. You will see the following options:

• Fullscreen: This shows an incoming call in the full-screen Phone app.

• Pop-up: This shows incoming calls as pop-ups at the screen's top.

• Mini pop-up: This displays incoming calls as a smaller pop-up.

• Keep calls in pop-up: If you activate this option, calls will be kept as pop-ups after they have been answered.

Manage calls

Your calls are stored in a call log. You can use voicemail, block numbers, and set up speed dials.

Call log

The numbers of received, missed, or dialed calls are stored in the Call log.

◦ Go to Phone > Recents. A list of your recent calls will be displayed. The name of the caller will be displayed if it is saved in your Contact's list.

Save a contact from a recent call

Make use of recent call info to update or create your contact list.

1. Go to 🅒 Phone > Recents.

2. Tap the call having the info you want to save to your Contact list, then tap Add to contacts.

3. Tap either Update existing contact or Create new contact.

Delete call records

To erase Call log entries:

1. Go to 🅒 Phone > Recents.

2. Press and hold the call that you want to be erased from the Call log.

3. Tap 🗑 Delete.

Block a number

When you include a caller in your Block list, any other call from that caller will be sent to your voicemail. Also, messages from that number will not be received.

1. Go to 📞 Phone > Recents.
2. Tap the caller that you want to include in your Block list.
3. Tap ⓘ Details > 🚫 Block, and confirm when you are prompted to do so. You can edit your Block list via Settings. Go to 📞 Phone and tap More options > Settings > Block numbers.

Speed dial

To speed dial a number, you can assign a shortcut number to that number.

1. Go to 📞 Phone > Keypad > ⋮ More options > Speed dial numbers. The number screen of the Speed dial displays the saved speed dial numbers.

2. Tap an unassigned number.

- Tap ▼ Menu to choose a Speed dial number that is different from the next one in the sequence.
- The allocated number for voicemail is Number 1.

3. Type in a number or name, then tap 👤 Add from Contacts to allocate a contact to that number.

- You can see the selected contact in the number box of the Speed dial.

Make a call with Speed dial

You can make use of a speed dial to make a call.

○ Go to 📞 Phone, then touch and hold the Speed dial number.

- If the number of the Speed dial is

more than one digit long, input the first digits, then hold the last digit.

Remove a Speed dial number

You can erase an assigned Speed dial number.

1. Go to Phone, tap More options > Speed dial numbers.

2. Tap Delete located next to the contact that you want removed from Speed dial.

Emergency calls

You can dial your region's emergency telephone number whether there is network service in your phone or not. You can only make emergency calls if your phone has not been activated.

1. Go to Phone and input the emergency telephone number (911 in

North America) then tap 🕻 Call.

2. When making this type of call, you also have access to most of the in-call features.

💡 Even though the phone is locked, you can still dial the emergency number. This feature allows anybody to call for emergency with your phone. Only the features of the emergency call will be accessible when accessed from the locked screen. Other features will remain locked.

Phone settings

These settings let you modify the Phone app settings.

○ Go to 🕻 Phone, tap ⋮ More options > Settings.

Optional calling services

The following calling services maybe supported by your service plan and wireless carrier.

Place a multi-party call

You can make another call even while a call is in progress. This option differ depending on the carrier.

1. From the active call, tap ✛ Add call to dial the second call.

2. Dial the second number then tap 📞 Call. When the call has been answered:

• Tap ⊔ Swap to swap between the two calls.

• Tap the On hold number to toggle between the two calls.

• Tap ⇉ Merge to hear both callers

together (multi-conferencing).

Video calls

To make Video calls:
- Tap 📞 Phone, input a number, then tap 🟠 Duo call or 🎥 Video call or 🔵 Video call.

💡 Video call is not supported in all devices. The receiver has the option to either accept the video call or answer the call like a regular voice call.

Real Time Text (RTT)

When you are on a call, you can still type in real time with the other person.
You can make use of RTT when you are

calling an RTT supported phone or someone teletypewriter-supported device (TTY). The RTT icon will be displayed on all the incoming RTT calls.

1. Go to Phone, tap More options > Settings.

2. Tap Real time text to get the following options:

• RTT call button: Select a visibility option for the RTT call button.

• Always visible: Display the RTT call button during a call and also on the keypad.

• Use external TTY keyboard: When there is an external TTY keyboard connected, this option hides the RTT keyboard.

• TTY mode: Select the preferred TTY

mode for the keyboard that is being used

Samsung Health

Make use of Samsung Health™ to plan, and track different daily life aspects that contributes to your well-being. These include diet, sleep, physical activities, and more.

💡 Be aware that the information got from Samsung Health, this device or other related software is not intended for use in disease diagnostics, treatment, cure, or prevention.

The accuracy of the data and information given by this device and the related software may be influenced by certain factors such as the device settings, environmental conditions, specific activities performed while wearing or using the device, user-provided information/configuration, and other end-user interactions.

Before you start exercising

Although the Samsung health app is a wonderful exercise routine companion, it is best to see your doctor before you start exercising.

Moderate exercise like walking is safe, but health experts advise that you involve your physician before beginning an exercise routine, especially if you have the following health conditions:

- Heart disease; Diabetes, Asthma or lung disease; kidney or liver disease; and Arthritis.

Before you start your exercise program, ascertain from your doctor if you have symptoms of diseases related to lung, heart, or other serious conditions, like:

- Discomfort or pain in the neck, jaw, chest, or arms during physical activity;
- Loss of consciousness or Dizziness;
- Breathe shortness when resting, lying down, going to bed, or in mild exertion;
- Ankle swelling, mostly at night;
- Fast heartbeat, or heart murmur;
- Muscle pain when walking up a hill or upstairs goes away when resting.

It is advised that you consult your

physician before you engage in an exercise program. If you are pregnant or not sure of your health status, meet your doctors before starting an exercise routine.

Samsung Notes

Make use of Samsung Notes to create notes that contain images with footnotes, music, voice recordings, and text. Make use of social networking platforms to easily share your notes.

Create notes

Add images, recordings, texts, and others.

1. Go to Samsung Notes, tap . Add.
2. Create content using the text options.

Voice recordings

Create voice recording annotations just for meetings or lectures. Take notes as you record audios. The playback is synchronized to scroll to the corresponding text.

1. Go to Samsung Notes, tap . Add.
2. Tap Insert > Voice recordings.
3. Create contents while the audio is being recorded using the text option.

Edit notes

Edit the notes that you created.

1. Go to Samsung Notes, tap a note to see it.
2. Tap Edit and make necessary changes.
3. Tap More options to get the

following:

- Share: Select a file type, then share the note.
- Save as file: Decide how to save the note, either as PDF, Microsoft PowerPoint, text file, Samsung Note, or Microsoft Word.
- Sort pages: Add, cut, delete and copy pages.
- Page template: Apply a template to either some pages or all the pages.
- Background color: Apply a page color.
- Add to favorites/Remove from favorites: In the notes menu, these notes are saved as favorites in a favorite folder.
- Add tags/Edit tags: Make use of tags

to search for your notes easily.

- Finger drawing on/Finger drawing off: Activate finger drawing. If it is disabled, only the S Pen can be used in drawing (for Galaxy S21 Ultra 5G only).

4. When you are done, tap Back.

Notes options

You can manage, sort, or edit notes.

○ The following options are present in Samsung Notes:

- Import PDFs: Enter a PDF file in Samsung Notes.
- Search: Look for a keyword.
- More options:
- Edit: Choose the notes to delete, save as file, lock, share, or move.
- Sort: Change the organization mode

of the notes.

– View: Toggle between List, Grid, Simple list.

Notes menu

You can see your notes by category.

○ Go to Samsung Notes, tap Navigation drawer to get the following options:

• Settings: View the Samsung Notes app settings.

• All notes: View all the notes.

• Frequently used: This is quick access to the notes that are commonly used.

• Shared notebooks: View the notebooks that are shared with your contacts via your Samsung account.

• Trash: View notes that have been deleted for up to 15 days.

- Folders: View notes categorized by groups.
- Manage folders: Remove, add or organize groups.

Samsung Pay

Samsung Pay™ allows you to pay for goods and services using your device. You can make use of it almost any place where you can either tap or swipe your credit card. To do this, you must have a Samsung account.

○ Go to Samsung Pay, and tap Get started, then follow the prompts.

 As an added security mechanism, your debit and credit card info is stored on a cloud service. If you want to make use of the Samsung Pay app on different devices, you have to sign in to the app on all the devices and confirm your cards. The number of devices may be limited by some card issuers.

Use Samsung Pay

Make use of Samsung Pay by launching the app and holding your device over the card reader of the store.

1. Go to Samsun Pay, and choose the card that you want to pay with, then authorize the payments by inputting your Samsung Pay PIN or scanning your finger.

2. Hold your phone over the card reader of the store.

- A receipt will be sent to your registered email when the payment is complete.

💡 Ensure that the NFC feature of your device has been activated.

Quick access

Utilize Quick access to quickly open Samsung Pay from the Home screen, Screen off or Lock Screen.

1. Go to 🅿 Samsung Pay, tap ≡ Menu > Settings > Quick access.

2. Tap ● to activate the screen options. To make use of Quick access:

1. From any interface, swipe up from the screen's bottom.

• Your Quick access and payment card are displayed.

2. Drag down the card to exit Quick access.

Use gift cards with Samsung Pay

Send, redeem and purchase gift cards from a wide selection of your best retailers.

Visit samsung.com/us/samsung-pay/compatible-cards/#bank to see a list of supported gift card merchants and banks.

Secure your information

Samsung Pay is made with the best and recent security technology. It works on most recent Samsung Galaxy devices. You authorize payments with your PIN or fingerprint. Also, each transaction makes use of a unique token, ensuring that only your consent is required to authorize a payment.

Chapter 10: Messages

Connect with your contacts, utilizing the Message app to send emojis, share pictures or just say a quick hello.

 Go to Messages, tap Compose new message.

Message search

Use the search feature to quickly find a message.

1. From Messages, tap Search.
2. In the keywords in the Search field, then tap Search.

Delete conversations

You can delete your conversations to remove your conversation history.

1. Go to Messages, tap More options > Delete.

2. Tap the conversations to be deleted.

3. Tap 🗑 Delete all, and confirm when you are prompted.

Send SOS messages

If you are in an emergency, this feature allows you to send a message displaying your location to specific contacts.

1. Go to Settings > ⊙ Advanced features > Send SOS messages, and then tap ⬤ to enable this feature.

• Tap 3 or 4 times to select the number of times that pressing the Side key will send an SOS message.

Tap Auto call someone to select the contact to call automatically after sending an SOS message.

• Tap Attach pictures to add a picture

from your rear and front cameras.

- Tap Attach audio recording to add a five-second audio clip in your SOS message.

Tap Send message to, to add recipients by either choosing from Contacts or creating a new contact.

2. To send an SOS message, press the Side key fast either three or four times.

Message settings

Set up the multimedia and text message settings.

○ From Messages, tap More options > Settings.

Emergency alerts

The Emergency alerts warn you of imminent threats. Receiving an Emergency alert message does not come with any charge.

1. Go to Settings > Notifications > Advanced settings.

2. To customize the emergency alerts notifications, tap Wireless Emergency Alerts.

Start here

My Files

See and manage your device files. These include music, sound clips, images, and ideos. You can also see and manage the files that are saved to your accounts in the cloud.

File groups

The files that are stored in the device are

arranged in the groups listed below:

- Recent files: View the files that are recently accessed.
- Categories: View your files according to their type.
- Storage: View the files saved on your cloud accounts and device.
- Cloud accounts differ based on the services you signed up for.

- Analyze storage: See the items consuming your storage space.

My Files options

Make use of the My Files option to search, clear, and edit file history and others.

○ Go to My Files, to see the following options:

- Search: Look for a folder or file.

- ⋮ More options:

- Cloud service: Connect to an available carrier cloud service.

- Clear Recent files list: Delete the list of files recently accessed. You can only access this option when you open a file via My Files.

- Analyze storage: See the items consuming your storage space.

- Trash: Select whether to restore or remove the files that you deleted permanently.

- Settings: View the app settings.

- Contact us: Connect with Samsung Members (if it is supported by your carrier).

Chapter 11: Google apps

The following apps by Google may come preloaded on your device. Besides you can download apps from the Google Play™ store.

Chrome

Surf the internet using Chrome™ and take your bookmarks, web address bar, and open tabs, from your computer to your mobile device.

Drive

Open, rename, share and view files that are stored in the cloud account of your Google Drive™.

Duo

Make video calls.

Gmail

Receive and send emails using Google's web-based email service.

Google

Locate contents online with the tools that learn areas of your interest.

Enable your personalized feed to get contents customized for you.

Google Pay

Use Google Pay™ to make payments using your Android phone at recognized stores and within certain mobile apps.

**Maps**

Get location-based info as well as directions. To make use of Google Maps, you must activate location services.

Photos

Save and automatically backup your videos and pictures to your Google Account using Google Photos™.

▶ Play Movies & TV

Watch TV shows and movies that you purchased from Google Play. You can also see videos that are saved on your device.

Play Store

Search the Google Play Store to see new apps, games, magazines, TV shows, books, and movies.

**YouTube**

Watch and upload YouTube™ videos using your device.

YT Music

Stream and search for artists, albums and playlists, via YouTube Music.

Notifications

• View and control your phone's notifications using your computer.

• Isolate notifications from individual apps.

• Get a Windows prompt notifying you of a new notification.

App mirroring

- Use your computer to live stream your phone's screen.
- Carry out phone interactions using the mouse and keyboard.
- Use the Windows Accessibility feature.

Connect your device to your Pc

1. Navigate to Settings > ⚙ Advanced features > Link to Windows.
2. Connect your phone to your computer by carrying out the displayed prompts.

💡 Know that you can also utilize the Quick Settings menu to enable this feature.

Samsung DeX

Link your phone to a TV or Computer to have a better multitasking experience.

• Transfer DeX to your TV and still make use of your device or convert your phone to a trackpad.

• Wirelessly connect to a monitor or TV. Alternatively, you can make use of an HDMI cable.

• For easy and fast transfer of files, install DeX on your computer.

1. Navigate to Settings > ⚙ Advanced features > Samsung DeX.
2. Tap ⬤ to enable this feature.
3. To link your PC or TV to your phone,

follow the prompts displayed in your device.

• Download the DeX app to your PC if the connection is to a computer. Visit samsungdex.com to get it.

Continue apps on other devices

This feature lets you answer and make calls and text messages from other Galaxy devices in which your Samsung account is signed in.

1. Navigate to Settings > Advanced features > Continue apps on other devices.

2. Tap to enable this feature. It will connect automatically.

3. Sign in to your Samsung account on the other Galaxy devices.

Transfer your contacts from your device to your Samsung account to enable you to access them on all the registered devices.

Chapter 12: Camera

Enjoy a variety of pro-grade lenses and pro video settings and modes.

- Navigate to Apps > Camera.

💡 If Quick Launch is activated, press the Side key two times to access the Camera app.

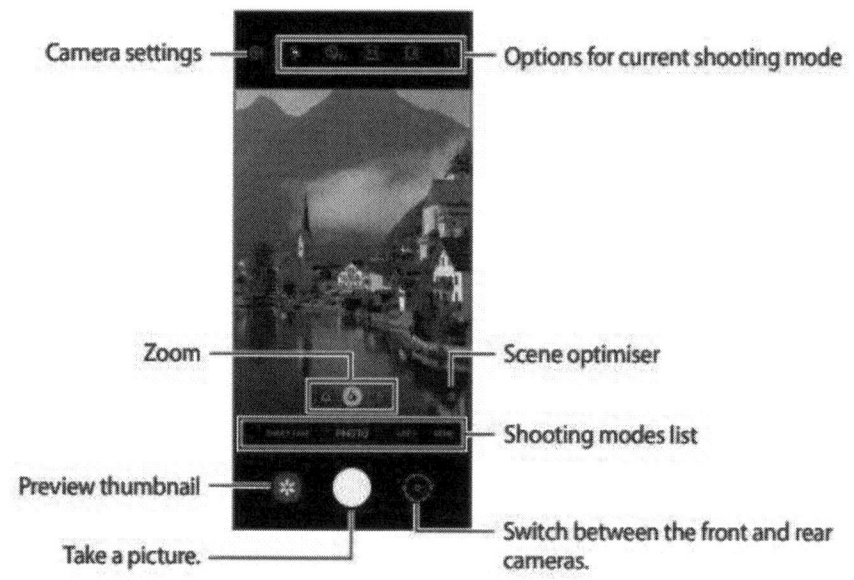

Navigate the camera screen

Take incredible pictures with the rear and front cameras of your device.

1. Go to ◉ Camera, and configure your shots with the following options:

• Tap the location to focus on the screen.

– Anytime you tap on the screen, a brightness scale will be displayed. Adjust this brightness by dragging the slider.

• Swipe the screen down or up to quickly switch between the rear and front cameras.

• Swipe either left or right to go to a different shooting mode.

• Tap ⚙ Settings to change the camera settings.

2. Tap ○ Capture.

Configure shooting mode

Let the camera determine your best picture mode or select from the different available modes.

○ Go to Camera, and swipe left or right to change the shooting modes.

• Single take: Take many pictures and video clips from multiple angles.

• Photo: Let the camera determine the best picture settings.

• Video: Let the camera determine the best video settings.

• More: Make your choice from other available shooting modes. To add or remove modes from the shooting modes tray located at the Camera screen bottom, Tap Add.

- AR Doodle: Include handwritings or line drawings to enhance your videos. The AR Doodle keeps track of spaces and faces to make them move as you move.
- Pro: While taking pictures, adjust the white balance, color tone, exposure value, and ISO sensitivity manually.
- Panorama: Take photos in either a vertical or horizontal direction to create a linear picture.
- Food: Take images that emphasize food's definitive colors.
- Night: Make use of this mode to capture low-light pictures without making use of the flash.
- Portrait: For portrait pictures, this mode adjusts your picture's background.
- Portrait video: For portrait videos, this mode adjusts your

video's background.

‒ Pro video: While recording videos, this mode manually adjust the white balance, exposure value, ISO sensitivity, and color tone.

‒ Super slow-mo: This mode records videos at a very high frame for high-quality slow-motion viewing. Even after recording, you can still play a certain section of the videos in slow motion.

‒ Slow-motion: Record high frame rate videos for slow-motion viewing.

‒ Hyperlapse: Record videos at different frame rates to make a video time-lapse. The frame rate will be automatically adjusted based on the device's movement and recorded scene.

‒ Director's view: Get access to

advanced features like changing between different rear camera lenses, locking unto a subject that is in view and others.

AR Zone

Gain access to all the Augmented Reality (AR) features together.

○ Navigate to Camera > More > tap AR Zone. The following features will be displayed:

• AR Emoji Camera: Make use of the camera to make your My Emoji avatar.

• AR Doodle: Add handwriting and line drawings to your environment. The AR Doodle keeps track of spaces and faces so that they can move as you move.

• AR Emoji Studio: Make use of AR tools to make and customize your My

Emoji avatar.

- AR Emoji Stickers: Add AR stickers to your My Emoji avatar.

Deco Pic: Decorate images or videos in real-time using the camera.

Scene optimizer

Adjust the contrast, exposure, and white balance automatically based on what the camera frame detects so that you can capture beautiful pictures.

○ Navigate to Camera > Photo > Scene optimizer.

Note that the Scene optimizer is available only for the rear camera. What the camera detects determines the automatic change of the Scene optimizer's icon. These changes occur when shooting nature shots or ☾ when taking pictures in a dark environment.

Single take

Capture more detail in each shot by taking both videos and images simultaneously. This shooting mode makes use of AI to make top quality videos and images from different angles. The number of videos and images may differ.

1. Navigate to Camera, and swipe to Single take.

2. Tap 10s and choose an option for your timer.

3. Tap Record, then pan around the scene to get different views and angles. The pictures and videos will be saved in

the Gallery app as a single entity

Space Zoom

Take pictures with magnification size of up to 100, having accuracy and clarity (the zoom options may differ by model).

1. Navigate to 🔘 Camera, tap the shortcut for Zoom and choose a magnification setting.

• When you are taking photos in higher magnifications, make your target to be in the frame's center, then tap 🔘 Zoom lock for a quick and accurate zoom focusing (for Galaxy S21 Ultra 5G only).

2. Tap ⭕ Capture.

Record videos

Use your device to record sleek lifelike videos.

1. Go to Camera, and swipe left or right to change the mode of shooting to Video.

2. Tap Record to start recording a video.

- Tap Capture to snap a picture as you are recording.

- Tap Pause to temporarily stop recording. Then tap Resume to continue the recording.

3. Tap Stop when you are done with the recording.

Director's view

Produce videos having fluid transitions between their camera angles. Record simultaneously from both the rear and front cameras. Also enable capturing with Split view or Picture-in-picture.

1. Go to Camera > More > Director's view.

2. Tap View then type to switch between Split view, Picture-in-picture, and Single views.

3. Tap Record.

• Centralize your subject and tap any of the windows that are available to change to another lens.

– Tap if the windows are invisible.

• Swipe the screen either down or up to toggle between the rear and front cameras.

4. Tap ▪ Stop when you are done recording.

Zoom-in mic

In Video mode, you can minimize the background noise by increasing the sound volume being recorded as you zoom into the source of audio. You cannot make use of this feature with the front camera or other video modes.

1. Navigate to 📷 Camera > ⚙ Settings.

2. Go to Advanced recording options > Zoom-in mic, and tap ⬤ to enable.

3. Tap ‹ Back to go back to the main screen of the Camera.

4. Change the shooting mode to Video by Swiping.

5. Tap ◉ Record to start recording.

6. To zoom in or out on the source of audio, bring your fingers apart or together on the screen. The icon of the microphone shows the amplification level that is applied.

Camera settings

Utilize the settings menu and the icons displayed on the main screen of the camera to set up the settings of your camera.

○ To get the following features, navigate to 🅒 Camera > ⚙ Settings:

Intelligent features

- Scene optimizer: This feature automatically adjusts the image color settings to align with the subject in view.

- Shot suggestions: Get on-screen instructions for help on shooting great shots.
- Scan QR codes: This feature automatically detects any QR code when making use of the camera.

Pictures

- Swipe Shutter button to: To feature allows you to decide whether to create a GIF or take a burst shot. To do this, shutter-swipe to the nearest edge.
- Format and advanced options: Select

a file format and other options for saving.

− HEIF pictures: Store images as pictures with high efficiency to save space. Not all sharing sites are compatible with this format.

− RAW copies: Save RAW and JPEG picture copies shot in Pro mode.

− Ultra-wide shape correction: This automatically corrects picture distortions shot using the ultra-wide lens.

Selfies

- Use wide-angle for group selfies: This automatically switches to a wide angle when there are more than two people in a selfie.
- Save selfies as previewed: This store selfies the way they appear in the

preview without having to flip them.

• Selfie color tone: Configure your selfie's color tone to either Bright or Natural.

Videos

• Advanced recording options: Improve the quality of your videos with the advanced recording formats.

– High efficiency videos: To save space, record your videos in the HEVC format. Not all video sharing sites or devices are compatible with this format.

– HDR10+ videos: Record videos in HDR10+ to optimize the videos. The playback devices must be HDR10+ video compatible.

– Zoom-in mic: While recording videos,

this feature matches the camera zoom to the mic zoom.

- Video stabilization: This enables the anti-shake feature to steady the focus when the camera is in motion.

Useful features

- Auto HDR: This captures more details in your shot's dark and bright areas.
- Tracking auto-focus: This keeps in focus an object that is in motion.
- Grid lines: This showcases the grid lines of the viewfinder to Display viewfinder grid lines to help compose a picture or video.
- Location tags: This pins a GPS location tag to your videos and pictures.
- Shooting methods:

- Press the Volume keys to: Record videos, control system volume, take photos, or zoom.
- Voice commands: To take photos with keywords.
- Floating shutter button: Include another shutter button that moves freely on the screen.
- Show palm: Stretch put your palm to face the camera to quickly take your picture.
• Settings to keep: Decide whether to launch the Camera with selfie angle, filters, or the same shooting mode as the last time.
• Shutter sound: Play a sound when taking a shot.
• Vibration feedback: Activate vibrations in the Camera app when

tapping the screen.

- Reset settings: Reset the settings of the Camera.
- Contact us: Make use of Samsung Members to Contact Samsung support if it is supported by your carrier.
- About Camera: See the software and app information.

Chapter 13: Gallery

Navigate to the Gallery to see all the media files stored on your device. You can see, manage, and edit videos and pictures.

○ Go to Apps, tap ✱ Gallery.

View pictures

You can see the images saved on your phone via the Gallery app.

1. Navigate to ✱ Gallery > Pictures.

2. Tap a picture to see it. To see other videos and pictures, swipe either right or left.

• Tap Bixby Vision to make use of Bixby Vision on the currently displayed image.

• To tag pictures as a favorite, tap

Add to Favorites.

- To see the following features, tap ⋮ More options:

‒ Details: See and edit the picture's info.

‒ Set as wallpaper: Make a picture your wallpaper.

‒ Copy to clipboard: Copy an image for pasting in another app.

‒ Move to Secure Folder: Move the image to a Secure Folder.

‒ Print: Send the image to a connected printer.

Edit ictures

Improve the quality of your pictures using the editing tools of your Gallery.

1. Navigate to ✹ Gallery > Pictures.

2. Tap an image to see it, then tap ✎ Edit to get the following options:

- Transform: Crop, Flip, Rotate, or make other changes to the picture's appearance.

- Filters: Add a color effect.

- Tone: Adjust the exposure, contrast, brightness, and more.

- Stickers: Overlay animated or illustrated stickers.

- Draw: Add hand-drawn content or handwritten text.

- Text: Add a text to the picture.

- Portrait: Enhance facial features and skin tones.

- Auto adjust: Apply adjustments automatically to improve the image.

- Revert: Reverse the applied changes to their original mode.

3. Tap Save when you are done.

Play video

See the videos that are saved on your device. You can see their details as well as save a video as favorites.

1. Navigate to ⊛ Gallery > Pictures.

2. Tap a video to see it. To see other videos or pictures, swipe right or left.

- To tag a video as a favorite, tap ♡ Add to Favorites. The video will be included as Favorites under the tab for Albums.

- To get access to the following option, tap ⋮ More options:

   - Details: See and edit video info.

- Set as wallpaper: Make the video a Lock screen wallpaper.
- Move to Secure Folder: Include a video in your Secure Folder.

3. Tap ▶ Play video to play a video.

Video enhancer

Improve your video's picture quality to enjoy more vivid and brighter colors.

1. Navigate to Settings > Advanced features > Video enhancer.
2. Tap ⬤ to activate this feature.

Edit video

Edit the videos saved on your device.

1. Navigate to ⊙ Gallery > Pictures.
2. Tap a video to see it.
3. Tap ✎ Edit to make use of the

following tools:
- ▶ Play: Preview an edited video.
- ✂ Trim: Cut some video segments.
- 🗘 Transform: Flip, rotate, crop, or make other video changes.
- ⊛ Filters: Add a visual effect to the video.
- 🙂 Sticker: Overlay animated or illustrated stickers.
- ✏ Draw: Draw on a video.
- T Text: Add texts to a videos.
- 🙂 Portrait: Enhance facial features and skin tones.
- ⊙ Speed: Adjust the speed of play.
- ♪ Audio: Add background music and adjust the volume levels of the video.

4. Tap Save, and then confirm when

instructed to do so.

Share pictures and videos

Share videos and images via the Gallery app.

1. Navigate to ⊛ Gallery > Pictures.
2. Tap More options > Edit and choose the videos or images to be shared.
3. Tap ⋖ Share, then select the connection or app you want to use for the sharing process and follow the displayed instructions.

Delete videos and pictures

Delete the videos and pictures saved on your device.

1. Navigate to ⊛ Gallery, > ⋮ More options > Edit.

2. Tap videos and images to select them.

3. Tap Delete, and confirm when instructed to do so.

Group like images

Organize similar videos and images in the Gallery.

1. Navigate to Gallery > Group similar images.

2. Tap Ungroup similar images to go back to the default Gallery view.

Take a screenshot

Capture a screenshot. In the Gallery app, your device will automatically create an album for Screenshots.

○ From any screen, press and release the Volume down and Side keys.

Capturing a screenshot via Palm swipe

Swipe your hand's edge across an image to capture a screenshot of it. Do this from side to side while in contact with the screen.

1. Navigate to Settings > ○ Advanced features > Motions and gestures >Palm swipe to capture.
2. Tap ● to activate the feature.

Screenshot Settings

Modify the settings of the screenshot.

○ Navigate to Settings > ⚙ Advanced features > Screenshots and screen recorder.

● Screenshot toolbar: Display more options after taking a screenshot.

● Hide navigation and status bars: This hides the navigation or status bars of screenshots.

● Delete shared screenshots: This automatically erases screenshots after they have been shared via the toolbar.

● Screenshot format: Select if you want your screenshots to be stored as PNG or JPG files.

Screen recorder

Write notes, record activities, and record your video overlay to be shared with family and friends.

1. Navigate to Quick Settings > Screen recorder > Start recording.

2. Before it begins recording, a three-second countdown will run. You can start recording immediately by skipping the count down.

- Tap Draw to screen draw.
- Tap Pointer to display a screen icon when making use of your S Pen (for Galaxy S21 Ultra 5G only).
- Tap Selfie video to add a front camera recording.

3. Tap Stop to finish recording. These are stored automatically in your Gallery's Screen recording album.

Screen recorder settings

Control the screen recorder's quality and

sound settings.

- Navigate to Settings > Advanced features > Screenshots and screen recorder.
- Sound: Select the sound to record when making use of the screen recorder.
- Video quality: Choose a resolution. You will need more memory space if you choose a higher resolution for better quality.
- Selfie video size: To set the video overlay size, drag the slider.

Chapter 14: Multi-window

Use many tasks simultaneously. The apps that are Multi window™ supported can be displayed concurrently on a split-screen. You can adjust their window sizes and also switch between the apps.

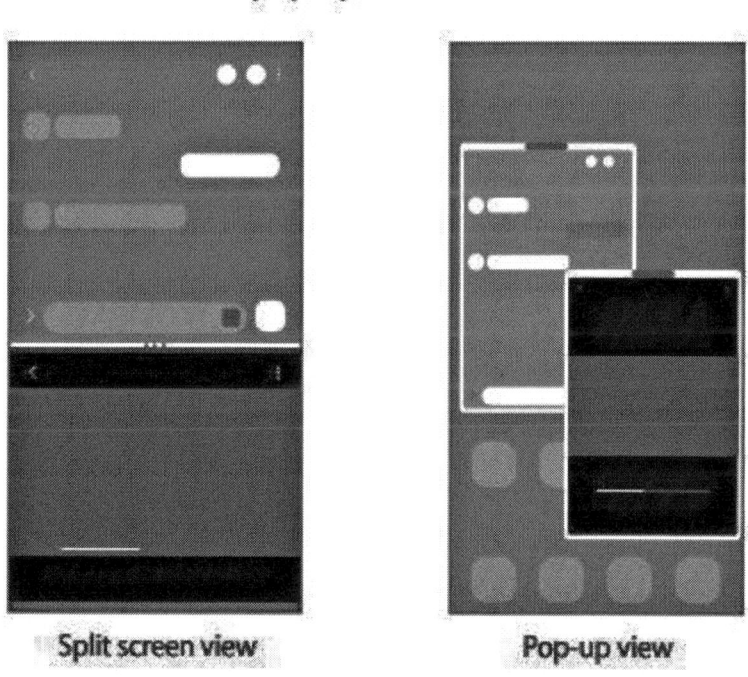

Split screen view   Pop-up view

1. Navigate to ≡ Recent apps.

2. Tap the icon of the app, then tap Open in the split-screen view.

3. Tap another app located in the other window to include it in the split-screen view.

- Drag the window border's center to adjust the size of the window.

Window controls

The Window controls manages the way the app windows are showcased in split screen view.

1. Resize the windows by dragging the center of the window border.

2. To get the following options tap the center of the window border:

- ↑↓ Switch window: Switch both

windows.

- **Add app combo to Edge panel:** Create and add the shortcut to an app pair to the App panel located at the edge of the screen.

Chapter 15: Settings

Access Settings

There are different methods of accessing the settings of your device.

● Swipe down from a Home screen and tap ⚙ Settings.

● Go to Apps, and tap ⚙ Settings.

Search for Settings

You can search for a setting if you are not sure of its location.

1. Go to Settings, and tap 🔍 Search, then input the keywords.

2. Tap a displayed entry access the setting.

Connections

Manage the connections between networks, your device and other devices.

Wi-Fi

You can access the internet without making use of your mobile data by connecting your device to a Wi-Fi network.

1. Go to Settings, and tap 📶 Connections > Wi-Fi, and then tap ⬤ to enable I Wi-Fi and scan for the networks available.

2. Tap a network, and input a password if it is required.

Connect to a hidden Wi-Fi network

You can still connect to a Wi-Fi network

that is not listed after a scan. To do this, just input the necessary information manually. Request the Wi-Fi administrator to give you the password and name of the network.

1. Go to Settings, and tap 📶 Connections > Wi-Fi, then tap ⬤ to switch on Wi-Fi.

2. Tap ➕ Add network located at the list's bottom.

3. Input the Wi-Fi network info:

• Network name: Input the network's exact name.

• Security: Choose a security option from the displayed list, then input the password if necessary.

• Advanced: Define other advanced

options, such as Proxy and IP settings.

4. Tap Save.

💡 Using your device's camera, tap the QR scanner button to scan a QR code and connect to a Wi-Fi network.

Advanced Wi-Fi settings

You can managed saved networks, look up the network addresses of your device and set up connections to different hotspots and Wi-Fi types. This feature may differ based on carrier.

1. Go to Settings, tap Connections > Wi-Fi, and then tap to turn on Wi-Fi.
2. Tap More options > Advanced.

- Switch to mobile data: When this is

enabled, your device will switch to mobile data when there is an unstable Wi-Fi connection. It will switch back to Wi-Fi when the network becomes stable again.

- Turn on Wi-Fi automatically: This switches the Wi-Fi on in frequently used locations on.
- Detect suspicious networks: Be notified when a suspicious activity happening on the current Wi-Fi network is detected.

- Show network quality info: This displays certain information of the network such as stability and speed.
- Wi-Fi power saving mode: Activate Wi-Fi traffic analysis to minimize battery usage.
- Network notification/Wi-Fi

notifications: Get notifications when there is a detected open network in range.

- Show Wi-Fi pop-up: This alerts you when there is an available Wi-Fi network while using an app.
- Manage networks: See the saved Wi-Fi networks and set them up to either reconnect or forget individual networks.
- Wi-Fi control history: View the apps that have switched on or off your Wi-Fi network recently.
- Hotspot 2.0: Automatically connect your device to a Wi-Fi network supporting Hotspot 2.0.
- Install network certificates: Install authentication certificates.

Wi-Fi Direct

Wi-Fi Direct makes use of Wi-Fi to share data between two or more devices.

1. Go to Settings, and tap Connections > Wi-Fi, then tap to switch on Wi-Fi.
2. Tap More options > Wi-Fi Direct.
3. To connect, tap a device, and follow the prompts.

Disconnect from Wi-Fi Direct

Disconnect your device from a Wi-Fi Direct device.

- Go to Settings and tap Connections > Wi-Fi > More options > Wi-Fi Direct. Tap a device to disconnect it.

Bluetooth

You can pair your device with other devices that have Bluetooth. These devices include the car's Bluetooth-enabled infotainment system and Bluetooth headphones. When both devices have been paired, you will not have to enter the passkey next time as the devices will remember each other.

1. Go to Settings, tap 🌐 Connections > Bluetooth, then tap ⬤ to turn on Bluetooth.

2. To connect, tap a device and follow the prompts.

💡TIP When sharing a file, tap 🔵 Bluetooth to make use of this feature.

Rename a paired device

To make a paired device easier to be remembered, you can simply rename it.

1. Go to Settings, tap Connections > Bluetooth, then tap to switch on Bluetooth.

2. Tap Settings located next to the name of the device, then tap Rename.

3. Input a new name, and tap Rename.

Unpair from a Bluetooth device

Unpairing your device from a Bluetooth device makes both devices no more recognizable to each other. You will have to pair them again to connect.

1. Go to Settings, tap Connections > Bluetooth, then tap to switch on Bluetooth.

2. Tap Settings located next to the

device, then tap Unpair.

Advanced options

You can find more Bluetooth features in the Advanced menu. This option may differ based on the carrier.

1. Go to Settings > 🛜 Connections > Bluetooth.

2. Tap ⋮ More options > Advanced or Advanced to see the following options:

• Sync with Samsung Cloud: Sync the files that are transferred through Bluetooth with your Samsung account.

• Phone name: Change Your device's name for Bluetooth connections.

• Received files: View a list of files received via Bluetooth.

- Music Share: Allow friends to play music on your Bluetooth headphones or speaker.
- Ringtone sync: Make use of the ringtone for calls for your device when you receive calls via a connected Bluetooth device.
- Bluetooth control history: See the apps that have recently made use of Bluetooth.

Dual audio

You can play your device audio on two connected Bluetooth audio devices.

1. Connect the Bluetooth audio devices to your device.
2. Navigate to the Notification panel and tap Media.
3. Under the Audio output, tap ✓ next

to the different audio devices to play audio in them (up to two devices).

NFC and payment

Near Field Communication (NFC) lets you communicate with another device without the use of a network connection. This technology is used by some payment apps and Android Beam. NFC needs to be supported on the device that you are transferring to. Also the distance between both devices should be within four centimeters.

○ Go to Settings, tap ◉ Connections > NFC and contactless payments, and then tap ● to switch on this feature.

Tap and pay

Using an NFC payment app, touch your

device to a compatible credit card reader to make payments.

1. Go to Settings, tap 🛜 Connections > NFC and contactless payments, and then tap ⬤ to switch on NFC.

2. Tap Contactless payments to view the default payment app.

- To make use of another payment app, tap an available app to select it.
- To make use of an open payment app, tap Pay with the currently open app.
- To make another payment service your default app, tap Others, and then select your preferred service.

💡 Samsung Pay makes use of the NFC technology. Switch this feature on to securely and quickly make payments with your device.

Airplane mode

Airplane mode switches of every network connection. These include mobile data, Bluetooth, calls, text, and Wi-Fi. You can still turn on Bluetooth and Wi-Fi in Settings or from the Quick Settings panel while the Airplane mode is active.

○ Go to Settings and tap 🛜 Connections > Airplane mode, then tap ⬤ to activate this feature.

Mobile networks

Make use of mobile networks to connect your device to available mobile networks so that you can make use of mobile data. The options may differ depending on the carrier.

- Go to Settings, tap Connections > Mobile networks.

• Mobile data: Enable the use of mobile data.

• International data roaming: Change the data, text, and voice settings for international roaming.

• Allow 2G service: Allow 2G device use in locations with low network coverage.

• Data roaming: Decide whether to let your device connect to mobile data while away from the network area of your carrier.

• Data roaming access: Setup mobile

network access when roaming.

- Roaming/Roaming state: Disable or enable data when roaming on other mobile networks.

- Signal strength: See the signal strength of your device.

- Enhanced Calling: Activate improved communication using LTE data.

- Network mode: Select the network modes to be used by your device.

- System select: If applicable in your carrier, you can change the CDMA roaming mode.

- Access Point Names: Select or add APNs, that have the network settings needed by your device to connect to your service provider.

- Network operators: Select your preferred and available networks.

- Mobile network diagnostics: Gather usage and diagnostic data for troubleshooting.

- Network extenders: Scan for cells that can expand your network connection.

☼ You can make use of these features to manage your connection settings and reduce your monthly bill.

Data usage

Check your current Wi-Fi and mobile data usage. Also, you can customize limits and warnings.

○ Go to Settings > 🛜 Connections > Data usage.

Turn on Data saver

Make use of a Data saver to minimize your data consumption by preventing certain apps from receiving or sending background data.

1. Go to Settings > Connections > Data usage > Data saver.
2. Tap to switch on Data saver.

• Tap allow to use data while Data saver is on to let some apps have unrestricted data usage, then tap located next to each app to next their restrictions.

Monitor mobile data

You can customize how your mobile data is accessed by setting restrictions and limits. These options may differ based on your carrier.

- Go to Settings > Connections > Data usage to see the following options:

• Mobile data: Use your plan's mobile data.

• International data roaming: Activate your mobile data services when internationally roaming.

• Mobile data only apps: Configure apps to use mobile data always and when your device is Wi-Fi connected.

• Alert me about data usage: Switch on alerts for when the usage of your mobile data reaches a certain specified amount.

• Mobile data usage: See the usage of mobile data for a long time. You can also see the total usage of data by apps.

- Billing cycle and data warning: Align with your carrier's billing date by changing the monthly date.

☼ Monitor your estimated data usage using these features.

Monitor Wi-Fi data

Customize the networks and their usage limits to restrict Wi-Fi data access.

1. Go to Settings, > 📶 Connections > Data usage.

2. Tap Wi-Fi data usage to see the data usage over Wi-Fi connections over certain time interval. You can also see the usage by apps as well as total usage.

Roaming data usage

You can monitor your data usage when you roam outside the network of your carrier.

1. Go to Settings > Connections > Data usage.

2. Tap Roaming data usage to see the usage of data when you are roaming.

Mobile hotspot

The Mobile hotspot makes use of your data plan to create a Wi-Fi network that is usable by many devices.

1. Go to Settings > Connections > Mobile hotspot and tethering > Mobile hotspot.

2. Tap to switch on the Mobile

hotspot.

3. Activate Wi-Fi on the devices to be connected, then choose the Mobile hotspot of your device. To connect, input the password of the Mobile hotspot.

• You can find the Connected devices listed under the heading Connected devices.

☼ Tap ▦ QR code to connect another device to the Mobile hotspot via QR code scanning instead of inputting a password.

Change the password of the Mobile hotspot

You can customize the password of your Mobile hotspot password so that you can easily remember it.

1. Navigate to Settings > Connections > Mobile hotspot and tethering > Mobile hotspot.

2. Tap the password, input a new password, then tap Save.

Configure mobile hotspot settings

You can customize the connection and security settings of your mobile hotspot.

1. Navigate to Settings, > Connections > Mobile hotspot and tethering > Mobile hotspot.

2. Tap Configure to see the following settings:

- Network name: See and change your Mobile Hotspot's name.
- Security: Select your Mobile hotspot security level.

- Password: If you select a security level that makes use of a password, you can both see and change it.
- Band: Choose any of the bandwidth options available.
- Advanced: Set up additional Mobile hotspot settings.

Auto hotspot

Automatically share your hotspot connection with other devices that are signed in to your Samsung account.

1. Go to Settings, > 🛜 Connections > Mobile hotspot and tethering > Mobile hotspot.
2. Tap Auto hotspot, then tap ⬤ to activate the feature.

Tethering

You can make use of tethering to share the internet connection of your device with other devices. This option may differ based on the carrier.

1. Go to Settings, > 🛜 Connections > Mobile hotspot, and tethering.

2. Tap any of the following options:

• Tap Bluetooth tethering to share the internet connection of your device Internet connection via Bluetooth.

• Connect your device to a computer through a USB cable, then tap USB tethering.

• Connect your device to a computer using an Ethernet adapter, then tap Ethernet tethering.

Nearby device scanning

Turn on Nearby device scanning to setup up fast connections to other available devices. If there are devices available for connection nearby, this feature will send you a notification.

1. Go to Settings > Connections > More connection settings > Nearby device scanning.

2. Tap to switch on the feature.

Connect to a printer

Establish a connection between your device and a printer via the same Wi-Fi network. This is to enable you to print images and documents from your device easily.

1. Navigate to Settings > Connections > More connection settings > Printing.

2. Tap Default print service, then tap ⋮ More options > Add a printer.

- If a plugin is required by your printer, tap ➕ Download plugin then follow the prompts to include a print service.

💡 Note that it is not all the apps that support printing.

Virtual Private Networks

A Virtual Private Network (VPN) lets you connect to a private secured network through your device. To do this, the connection info from your VPN administrator will be needed.

1. Go to Settings, > Connections > More connection settings > VPN.

2. Tap More options > Add VPN profile.

3. Input the information of the VPN network given to you by your network administrator, then tap Save.

Manage a VPN

Make use of the VPN settings menu to delete or edit a VPN connection.

1. Go to Settings, > Connections > More connection settings > VPN.

2. Tap Settings located next to a VPN.

3. Edit the VPN then tap Save, or tap

Delete to delete the VPN.

Connect to a VPN

It is easy to connect to and disconnect from a VPN once you have set it up.

1. Go to Settings, > 🛜 Connections > More connection settings > VPN.

2. Tap a VPN, input your log-in info, then tap Connect.

• To disconnect, tap the VPN, then tap Disconnect.

Private DNS

You can setup your device for a private host DNS connection.

1. Navigate to Settings, > 🛜 Connections > More connection settings > Private DNS.

2. Tap any of the options available options to set up a private DNS connection.

3. Tap Save.

Ethernet

If there is no available wireless network connection, you can make use of an Ethernet cable to connect your device to a local network.

1. Connect an Ethernet cable to your device.

2. Go to Settings > Connections > More connection settings > Ethernet, then follow the prompts.

 Note that an adapter (not included) is needed to connect your device to the Ethernet cable.

Network unlock

See the lock status of your device's network and check if your device can be unlocked for use on a different mobile network. This option may differ based on the carrier.

○ Go to Settings, > 🛜 Connections > More connection settings > Network unlock

To get the following options:

• Network lock status: see your device's current network lock status.

• Permanent unlock: Ask for a permanent network unlock so that you can make use of your device together with other service providers.

- Temporary unlock: Ask for a temporary network unlock so that you can make use of your device with other service providers.

Chapter 16: Sounds and vibration

You can control the vibration and sounds that are used for indication such as screen touches, notifications, and other interactions.

Sound mode

You can change the mode of your device sound without making use of the volume keys.

○ Go to Settings, tap 🔊 Sounds and vibration, then select a mode:

• Sound: Make use of the vibrations, sounds, and volume levels that you have chosen in Sound settings for your alerts and notifications.

- Vibrate while ringing: Configure your device to vibrate while ringing when you have a call.

• Vibrate: Make use of only vibration for alerts and notifications.

• Mute: Configure your device to be silent.

- Temporary mute: Set a time limit for your device to stay muted.

💡 Make use of the sound mode setting instead of the volume keys to use a different sound mode without losing the sound levels that you customized.

Mute with gestures

Turn over the device or cover the screen

to quickly mute sounds.

○ Go to Settings, > Advanced features > Motions and gestures > Mute with gestures, then tap ⬤ to enable.

Vibrations

You can control the way and time that your device vibrates.

1. Go to Settings, tap 🔊 Sounds, and vibration.
2. Tap any of the options to customize:

• Call vibration pattern: Select from already set call vibration patterns.

• Notification vibration pattern: Select from already set notification vibration patterns.

• Vibration intensity: Drag the sliders

to configure the levels of the vibration intensity for touch interactions, notifications, and calls.

Volume

Configure the volume level for notifications, media, call ringtones, and system sounds.

○ Go to Settings, > 🔊 Sounds and vibration > Volume, then drag the sliders for the different sound types.

💡 Note that you can adjust the volume using the Volume keys. When you press it, a pop-up menu will be displayed showing the current sound type and volume level. Simply tap the menu to adjust it and also drag the sliders to adjust the volume of other types of sound.

Use Volume keys for media

Control the sound volume of media by setting their default volume.

1. Go to Settings, > 🔊 Sounds and vibration > Volume.

2. Activate this feature by tapping Use Volume keys for media.

Media volume limit

Set a limit to your device's volume maximum output when making use of headphones(not included) or a Bluetooth speaker.

1. Go to Settings > 🔊 Sounds and vibration > Volume.

2. Tap ⋮ More options > Media volume limit.

3. Tap ⦿ to activate this feature.

- Drag the Custom volume limit slider to set the maximum volume output.
- Tap Set volume limit PIN to require a PIN to effect changes to the settings of the volume.

Ringtone

Select from already set sounds or add your own to customize your call ringtone.

1. Go to Settings, > 🔊 Sounds and vibration > Ringtone.

2. Listen to a ringtone preview by tapping it then select it, or ＋Add to

make use of an audio file as a ringtone.

Notification sound

Select a preset sound for all the notification alerts.

1. Navigate to Settings, > Sounds, and vibration > Notification sound.
2. Tap a sound to listen to its preview, then choose it.

Using the App settings menu, you can also make the notification sounds to be unique for different apps.

System sound

Select a sound theme to use for charging, Samsung Keyboard, touch interaction, changing the sound mode, and more.

○ Go to Settings, > Sounds and vibration > System sound and select an available option.

System sounds and vibration

Customize the vibrations and sounds of your device for actions such as device charging and screen tapping. The options may differ based on the carrier.

○ Navigate to Settings > 🔊 Sounds and vibration > System sound/vibration control to see the following options:

Sound

• Touch interactions: Play tones when you make selections by tapping or touching the screen.

• Screen lock/unlock: Play a sound when you unlock or lock the screen.

- Charging: Play a sound when the device is connected to a charger.
- Dialing keypad: Play a tone using the phone keypad to dial numbers.
- Samsung keyboard: Play a sound when using with the Samsung keyboard to type.

Vibration

- Touch interactions: Vibrate when you touch and hold items on the screen or when you tap navigation buttons.
- Dialing keypad: Vibrate when making use of the phone keypad to dial numbers.
- Navigation gestures: Vibrate when making use of gestures.
- Charging: Vibrate when there is a connected charger.
- Samsung keyboard: Vibrate when typing using the

Samsung keyboard.

• Camera feedback: Vibrate when zooming, changing shooting modes, taking pictures, and more.

Dolby Atmos

Enjoy the Dolby Atmos quality when you are playing media that is specifically mixed for Atmos. You may also access this feature using a connected headset.

○ Go to Settings > 🔊 Sounds and vibration > Sound quality and effects to get the following options:

• Dolby Atmos: Experience clear audio flowing around and above you.

• Dolby Atmos for gaming: Apply Dolby

Atmos that is gaming-optimized.

Equalizer

Manually change your audio settings or select an audio preset that is configured to different music genres.

1. Go to Settings,> 🔊 Sounds and vibration > Sound quality and effects.
2. Tap Equalizer to select a music genre.

UHQ upscaler

Improve the sound resolution of videos and music for a better listening experience. You can only access this feature with a connected headset.

1. Navigate to Settings > 🔊 Sounds and vibration > Sound quality

and effects.

2. Tap UHQ upscaler and select an enhancement option.

Adapt sound

Customize the sound for your ears to improve your listening experience.

1. Go to Settings, > 🔊 Sounds and vibration > Sound quality and effects > Adapt sound.

2. Tap Adapt sound for, to choose when the sound settings should be changed.

3. Tap your preferred sound profile, then tap ⚙ Settings to customize.

💡 Tap Personalize your sound to enable your device to select your best sound.

Separate app sound

You can configure an app to play only media sound on a headset or Bluetooth speaker different from other sounds such as notification. To make this feature available in the menu of the Audio device, you have to connect to a Bluetooth device.

1. Navigate to Settings, > 🔊 Sounds and vibration > Separate app sound.

2. Tap Turn on now to activate Separate app sound, then configure the following options:

• App: Select an app to play its sound on another audio device.

• Audio device: Select the audio device where the sound of the app should be played on.

Chapter 17: Notifications

You can streamline and prioritize the alerts of apps by choosing the app to send you notifications and how you should be notified.

Notification pop-up style

You can customize your notification extra settings and style.

○ Go to Settings, > Notifications, then select a pop-up style:

• Brief: Enable customized notification lighting styles, colors, and apps.

- Included apps: See brief notifications for your apps.

- Brief pop-up settings: Set the colors, and lighting style of the Edge and allow the notifications to be displayed even when the screen is not on.

- Detailed: Activate the default Samsung Notification settings.

Recently sent notifications

You can see an app list containing the apps that have sent you notifications under Recently sent notifications.

1. Go to Settings > ⭕ Notifications.
2. Tap any entry under Recently sent to set up the notification settings.
3. Tap More to view the expanded list.

Do not disturb

When switched on the Do not disturb mode lets you block notifications and sounds. You can set up exceptions for alarms, apps, and people. You can schedule events like meetings or sleep.

- Go to Settings > Notifications > Do not disturb and setup the following:
- **Do not disturb**: Enable Do not disturb to block notifications and sounds.
- **For how long?**: When manually enabled, you can set a default time for the Do not disturb mode.
- **Sleeping**: Set up a sleep schedule for Do not disturb mode.
- **Add schedule**: Set a new schedule to configure the times and days to regularly put your device in Do not disturb mode.
- **Calls, messages, and conversations**: Tap to enable the Do not disturb exceptions.

- Alarms and sounds: Enable vibrations and sounds and vibrations for events, reminders, and alarms, when Do not disturb mode is active.
- Apps: In the Do not disturb mode, you can add the apps that you want to be receiving notifications from.

Even though you did not activate the feature in their apps, you can still be receiving notifications for messages, calls and conversations.

- Hide notifications: View the options for customization to hide notifications.

Advanced settings

You can set up services and apps notifications.

○ Navigate to Settings > ◉ Notifications > Advanced settings.

• Show notification icons: Edit the number of notifications that will be displayed on the Status bar.
• Show battery percentage: Show your device current battery life on the Status bar.
• Notification history: Display snoozed and recent notifications.
• Conversations: See notifications for conversations. Press and hold the notification of a conversation to mark it as a priority, set it silent, or as alerting.
• Floating notifications: Activate floating notifications in either Smart or Bubbles pop-up view.

- Suggest replies and actions for notifications: Get related suggestions for message replies and notification actions.
- Notification reminders: Activate and customize regular notification reminders for selected services and apps. Stop the reminders by creating the notifications.
- App icon badges: Use the badges appearing on their icons to identify the apps that have active notifications. Tap to select whether or not badges display the number of unread notifications.

- Wireless Emergency Alerts: Customize emergency alert notifications.

Alert when the phone is picked up

You can configure the device to notify you about messages and missed calls by vibrating when you pick it up.

- To activate, go to Settings > Advanced features > Motions and gestures > Alert when phone picked up.

Chapter 18: Display

You can customize the font size, screen brightness, timeout delay, and many other display settings.

Dark mode

Dark mode lets you keep your eyes more comfortable at night by switching to a darker theme. It darkens notifications and bright or white screens.

○ Go to Settings, and ⚙ Display to get the following options:

● Light: Apply a light color theme to your device (default).

● Dark: Apply a dark color theme to your device.

● Dark mode settings: Customize where and when Dark mode

is applied.

− Turn on as scheduled: Setup Dark mode for either custom schedule or Sunset to sunrise.

Screen brightness

Adjust the brightness of the screen based on your personal preference or lighting conditions.

1. Go to Settings > ⚙ Display.
2. Customize options under Brightness:

• Set a custom brightness level by dragging the Brightness slider.

• Tap Adaptive brightness to automatically adjust the brightness of the screen brightness depending on the lighting conditions.

💡 You can make use of the Quick

settings panel to also adjust the brightness of the screen.

Motion smoothness

Increase the refresh rate of the screen to get more realistic animations and smoother scrolling.

1. Navigate to Settings, > ⚙ Display > Motion smoothness.

2. Tap an option, then tap Apply.

Eye comfort shield

The eye comfort shield feature may enable you to reduce eye strain and sleep better. Also, you can schedule it to automatically turn on or off.

- Go to Settings, > ⚙ Display > Eye comfort shield, and then select any of the following options:

- Tap ⬤ to activate this feature.
- Tap Adaptive to automatically adjust the color temperature of the screen based on the time of the day and your usage patterns.
- Tap Custom to set a schedule that will enable the Eye comfort shield.
- Tap Set schedule and select either Custom, Sunset to Sunrise or Always on.
- To set the filter opacity, drag the Color temperature slider to set the opacity.

Screen mode

Your device has different screen mode options that adjust the quality of the screen for different conditions. You can choose the mode that you prefer.

1. Go to Settings > ⚙ Display > Screen mode.

2. Tap an option to enable a different screen mode.

Font style and size

You can customize your device by changing the font style and size.

○ Go to Settings > ⚙ Display > Font size and style to get the following options:

- Tap Font style to select another font.

- Tap a font to choose it, or tap ➕ Download fonts to get more fonts from Galaxy Store.

- Tap Bold font to enable bold weight on all fonts.

- To adjust the text size, drag the font size slider.

Screen zoom

Adjust the zoom level for easier content viewing.

1. Go to Settings > ⚙ Display > Screen zoom.

2. To adjust the zoom level, drag the Screen zoom slider.

Screen resolution

You can save battery by lowering the resolution of the screen or sharpen the image quality by increasing it (for Galaxy S21 Ultra 5G only).

1. Navigate to Settings > ⚙ Display > Screen resolution.

2. Tap the resolution of your choice, then tap Apply.

Note that some apps may not support wither the lower resolution or the higher resolution and may close if you change the resolution.

Full screen apps

You can select the apps that you want to use in the full-screen mode.

○ Go to Settings > ⚙ Display > Full screen apps then tap apps to activate this feature.

Screen timeout

You can configure the screen to turn off after some time.

○ Go to Settings > ⚙ Display > Screen timeout, then tap a time limit to configure it.

Note that apart from Always On Display, the prolonged display of images that are not moving may lead to degraded image quality or permanent ghost-like afterimages. Switch
off the display screen when it is not in use.

Accidental touch protection

Avoid the detection of screen touch inputs when the device is in a bag, pocket, or a dark place.

○ Go to Settings > Display > Accidental touch protection to activate this feature.

Touch sensitivity

Boost the screen's touch sensitivity for

use with screen protectors.

○ To enable, navigate to Settings > ⚙ Display > Touch sensitivity.

Show charging information

Even though the screen is off, you can still see the estimated time for a full charge and the battery level.

○ Go to Settings, tap ⚙ Display > Show charging information to activate.

Screen saver

While charging or when the screen is off, you can still display photos or colors.

1. Go to Settings > ⚙ Display > Screen saver.
2. Select any of the following options:

- None: Do not show a screen saver.
- Colors: Tap the selector to show changing screen colors.
- Photo table: Display pictures in a photo table.
- Photo frame: Display pictures in a photo frame.
- Photos: Display pictures from your Google Photos account.

3. Tap Preview to see a demonstration of the Screen saver that you selected.

💡 To get more options, tap ⚙ Settings next to a feature.

Lift to wake

Lift the device to turn the screen on.

○ To activate this feature, navigate to Settings > ⚙ Advanced features >

Motions and gestures > Lift to wake.

Double-tap to turn on the screen

Instead of using the Side key, you can double-tap to turn on the screen.

○ To activate this feature, navigate to Settings, tap Advanced features > Motions and gestures > Double tap to turn on the screen.

Double-tap to turn off the screen

Instead of using the Side key, double-tap to turn off the screen.

○ To activate this feature, navigate to Settings > Advanced features > Motions and gestures > Double tap to turn off the screen.

Keep screen on while viewing

To turn the display on, make use of the front camera to detect when you are looking at the screen.

◦ Go to Settings > ⚙ Advanced features > Motions and gestures > Keep screen on while viewing, then tap ⬤ to activate this feature.

One-handed mode

You can accommodate operating the screen with one hand by changing its layout.

1. Navigate to Settings > ⚙ Advanced features > One-handed mode.
2. Tap ⬤ to activate the feature then choose any of the following options:
- Gesture: Swipe down in the center of

the screen's bottom edge.

- Button: Tap ⬜ Home twice quickly to reduce the display size.

Chapter 19: Lock Screen and Security

Set a screen lock to protect your data and secure your device

Screen lock types

Choose from the following types of screen lock which offers no, medium, or high, security: No, Password, PIN, Pattern, Swipe.

💡 Note that biometric locks are also to protect from unauthorized access to tour sensitive data and devices. To know more, see Biometric security.

Set a secure screen lock

It is ideal to secure your device using a secure screen lock (Password, PIN, or Pattern).

This is essential to configure and enable biometric locks.

1. Navigate to Settings > 🔒 Lock screen > Screen lock type then tap a secure screen lock (Password, PIN, or Pattern).

2. Tap ● to enable notifications to be displayed on the lock screen. The following options are present:

- Icons only: Show only the notification icons on the lock screen without details.
- Details: Display the details of notification on the lock screen.

- Hide content: Do not display notifications in the Notification panel.
- Notifications to show: Select the notifications to be displayed on the

Lock screen.

- Show on Always On Display: Show notifications on the Always on Display screen.

3. Setup the following screen lock options:

- Smart Lock: Automatically unlock your device anytime a trusted device or location is detected. For this feature to work, a secure screen lock is required.

- Secure lock settings: Setup your secure lock settings. For this feature to work, a secure screen lock is required.

- Always On Display: Activate the Always On Display screen.

Clock and information

You can set up the features that are displayed on the Lock screen, such as the clock and other useful info.

○ Navigate to Settings, > 🔒 Lock screen to get the following options:

• Wallpaper services: Allow more features like Dynamic lock screen and guide page.

• Clock style: Set the color and type of the Always on Display screen and the lock screen clock.

• Roaming clock: Display the time in your current location and your home time while roaming.

• Widgets: Activate widgets on the Always On Display screen and the Lock screen to get fast access to helpful information.

- Contact information: Display your contact info, such as your email address or phone number.
- Notifications: Choose the notifications to be displayed on the Always On Display screen and the Lock screen.
- Shortcuts: Choose the app shortcut to be added to the Lock screen.
- About Lock screen: Update the software of the Lock screen.

Google Play Protect

You can setup Google Play to check your device and apps and for threats and security risks.

○ Navigate to Settings > ⭕ Biometrics and security > Google Play Protect.

- Updates are automatically checked for.

Security update

You can quickly check the last security software update date. Also, you can check if there are any available newer update.

○ Navigate to Settings > ◯ Biometrics and security > Security update to view the latest security update that is installed and also check for a newer available update.

Find My Mobile

Allow your device to be tracked or locked online or even get its data remotely deleted to protect it from theft or loss. To do this, a Samsung Account is needed. Also, the Google location service must be switched on to make use of the Find My Mobile feature.

Switch Find My Mobile

You must turn the Find My Mobile feature and customize its settings before you can make ise of it. For remote device accessing, visit findmymobile.samsung.com.

1. Navigate to Settings > Biometrics and security > Find My Mobile.

2. Tap to activate Find My Mobile, then log in to your Samsung account. The following options are present:

• Remote unlock: Let Samsung store your password, pattern or PIN, pattern, to allow you remotely control or unlock your device.

• Send last location: When the battery level of your device is below a certain level, this feature relays the last location of your device to the Find My Mobile server.

Samsung Pass

Make use of Samsung Pass to gain access to your preferred services via the biometric data. Ro makes use of the Samsung Pass, you must sign in to your Samsung account.

1. Go to Settings > ⚙ Biometrics and security > Samsung Pass.
2. Sign in to your Samsung account and include your biometric data.

Secure Folder

On your device, you can create a secure folder to restrict others from accessing your private apps and contents.

To configure and make use of the Secure folder, you must sign in to your Samsung account.

◌ Navigate to Settings > ◯ Biometrics and security > Secure Folder and follow the prompts to protect your content on your device.

Secure Wi-Fi

Get more privacy protection when you are using unsecured Wi-Fi networks. To set up and use the Secure Wi-Fi, you must sign in to your Samsung account.

◌ Navigate to Settings > ◯ Biometrics and security > Secure Wi-Fi and follow the prompts to set up privacy protection.

Private Share

Share your files privately, prevent the receivers from sharing them and set dates of expiration. Utilize blockchain technology to keep your data safe.

◌ Navigate to Settings > ◯ Biometrics and security > Private share, and follow the prompts to include files.

Samsung Blockchain Keystore

Manage the private keys of your blockchain. The availability of this feature is based on your carrier.

1. Navigate to Settings > ◯ Biometrics and security > Samsung Blockchain Keystore.
2. Follow the prompts to set up or import a new cryptocurrency wallet.

Install unknown apps

You can permit the installation of unknown third-party apps from certain sources.

1. Navigate to Settings > ⭕ Biometrics and security > Install unknown apps.

2. Tap a source or app, then tap Allow from this source.

💡 The installation of third-party apps could make your data and device vulnerable to threats.

Password for factory data reset

You can request a password to factory-reset your device.

The availability of this feature is dependent on your carrier.

○ Navigate to Settings > ⭕ Biometrics and security > Other security settings >

Set up/change password then input a password.

Set up SIM card lock

You can lock your SIM card using a PIN. This prevents unauthorized use of the SIM card in another device. The availability of this feature is dependent on your carrier.

- Navigate to Settings > ⚪ Biometrics and security > Other security settings > Set up SIM card lock then follow the prompts.
- Tap Lock SIM card to enable this feature.
- Tap Change SIM card PIN to create another PIN.

View passwords

You can briefly see your password characters in their field as you type.

○ Navigate to Settings > ◯ Biometrics and security > Other security settings > Make passwords visible to enable this feature.

Device administration

You can give your device administrative access to certain apps and security features.

1. Navigate to Settings > ◯ Biometrics and security > Other security settings > Device admin apps.

2. Turn any option to a device administrator by tapping it.

Credential storage

You can manage your device trusted security certificates, that verify servers' identity for secure connections.

○ Navigate to Settings > ⭕ Biometrics and security > Other security settings to get the following options:

• Storage type: Select a storage location for credential contents.

• View security certificates: Display installed certificates in your device's ROM.

• User certificates: View user certificates for device identification.

• Install from device/phone storage: Install a new certificate from storage.

• Clear credentials: Delete credential contents from the device and reset the password.

Advanced security settings

Set up advanced security settings using these options for better device protection.

○ Navigate to Settings > ⭕ Biometrics and security > Other security settings to get the following options:

• Trust agents: Allow device that you trust to perform certain actions when they are connected.

− You can only see this option when a lock screen is switched on.

• Pin windows: Pin an app on the screen of your device screen. This restricts access to other device features.

• Security policy updates: Secure your device by searching for security updates.

Permission manager

Certain apps can access features in your device if you permit them, such as location, microphone, or camera when they are functioning in the background. You can configure your device to inform you when this happens.

1. Navigate to Settings > Privacy > Permission manager.

2. Tap a category, and tap an app to choose the permissions to be notified about.

💡 A dialogue box will request your permission for access to certain features when using some apps for the first time.

Samsung Privacy

Anytime you are having technical issues with your device, you can send your device diagnostic information to Samsung.

1. Navigate to Settings, tap Privacy.
2. To customize, tap the following under Samsung :

• Samsung Privacy: View the privacy info of amsung.

• Customization Service: Permit Samsung to provide customized recommendations and content.

• Send diagnostic data: Whenever you are having technical issues, send your device diagnostic information to Samsung.

Location

Location services make use of Wi-Fi, mobile network, and GPS to ascertain your device location.

1. Navigate to Settings, tap Location.
2. Tap to switch on Location Services.

💡Certain apps require the location services to be switched on for them to be fully functional.

App permissions

Setup permissions for apps requesting access to your location information.

1. Navigate to Settings > Location > App permissions.
2. Tap an app and select the location

permissions to grant it. The options differ by app.

Improve accuracy

Activate other location scanning tools.

1. Navigate to Settings > 🌐 Location > Improve accuracy.

2. Tap the connection method to remove or add from location services:

• Wi-Fi scanning: Permit services and apps automatically scan for Wi-Fi networks, even if the Wi-Fi is switched off.

• Bluetooth scanning: Permit apps to automatically scan for and connect to nearby Bluetooth-enabled devices, even if the Bluetooth is switched off.

Recent location requests

See the apps that requested for your location.

1. Navigate to Settings > Location.
2. Tap to switch on Location Services.
3. Tap any entry under the Recent location requests to see the app's settings.

Location services

Location services save and make use of your device's most recent location data. Some apps can utilize this data to enhance your search results based on your visited locations.

1. Navigate to Settings > Location.
2. Tap any entry under Location services to see the usage of your location information.

Chapter 20: Accounts

You can manage and connect to your accounts. These include Samsung account, Google account, social media platforms, and email.

Add an account

You can include and synchronize all your social networks, video and image sharing, and email accounts.

1. Navigate to Settings > ⚙ Accounts and backup > Manage accounts > ➕ Add account.
2. Tap any of the account types.
3. Follow the displayed prompts to input your credentials and configure

the account.

● Tap Auto-sync data to activate account automatic updates.

Account settings

Every account has its custom settings. Besides, you can set up a common setting for the same type of accounts. The available features and account settings differ between the account types.

○ Navigate to Settings > 🔘 Accounts and backup > Manage accounts.

Remove an account

You can delete accounts from your device.

1. Navigate to Settings > Accounts and backup > Manage accounts.

2. Tap the account you want to remove then tap Remove account.

Backup and restore

You can set up your device to back up data to your accounts.

Samsung account

You can enable info backup to your Samsung account. The availability of this feature is dependent on your carrier.

○ Navigate to Settings Accounts and backup > Backup and restore for the options under Samsung Cloud:

• Back up data: Configure your

Samsung account for data backup.

- Restore data: Restore your backup data using your Samsung account.

Google Account

You can enable Google Account info backup.

1. Navigate to Settings > ⊚ Accounts and backup.
2. Tap Backup data under Google Drive.

External storage transfer

You can make use of a USB storage device to back up your data or make use of Smart Switch to restore backup data.

○ Navigate to Settings > ⊚ Accounts

and backup > External storage transfer.

Google settings

You can set up the Google settings of your device. The available options are dependent on your Google Account.

○ Go to Settings, tap Google, and choose an option to customize.

Chapter 21: Device Maintenance

See the status of the battery, memory, and storage of your device. Also, you can automatically optimize the system resources of your device.

Quick optimization

The quick optimization feature improves the performance of your device via the following actions:

• Singling out the apps that use undue battery power and clearing unneeded memory items.

• Deleting files that are not necessary and closing the background apps.

• Malware scanning.

To make use of the quick optimization

feature:

○　Navigate to Settings > ⚙ Battery and device care > Optimize now.

Battery

See how your different activities use up your battery power.

○　Navigate to Settings > ⚙ Battery and device care > Battery to get the following options:

• Usage since last full charge: See your recent battery usage by service, app, and time.
• Power saving mode: To save battery life, turn off Motion smoothness, location

checking, syncing, and limit background network usage. Enable the power saving options and select from the additional options to save more battery power.

• Background usage limits: See the apps that you do not normally use to limit their battery use. Tap Put unused apps to sleep to disable this feature.

• Wireless power-sharing: Use the battery of your device to enable wireless charging of supported devices.

• More battery settings:

– Adaptive battery: Limit the usage of battery for apps that you do not frequently use.

– Enhanced processing: Speed up data processes for most asking games and apps. This option makes use of more battery power.

- Show battery percentage: Show the percentage of the battery charge in the status bar next to the battery icon.

- Show charging information: Display the battery level and the estimated time until a full charge when the Always On Display is either not shown or off.
- Fast charging: Disable or enable the fast charging cable when it is connected to a compatible charger.
- Super fast charging: Disable or enable super fast charging whenever your device is connected to a compatible charger.
- Fast wireless charging: Disable or enable fast wireless charging whenever you are making use of a compatible

charger. Disable this option to prevent the noise of the fan when charging wirelessly.

Storage

See the detailed usage of your storage by file type and category and also your device storage capacity.

○ Navigate to Settings > ◉ Battery and device care > Storage.

• Tap a category to see and manage the files.

Memory

Check the available memory space. You can close the apps running in the background to reduce the memory usage so to speed up your device.

○ Navigate to Settings > ⚙ Battery and device care > Memory. The available and used memory will be displayed.

• Tap Clean now to free up enough memory space.

• Tap View more to see the full apps list and the services using the memory. Tap ⊙ to either exclude or include these services and apps.

• Tap Apps not used recently to display services and apps that are included in this group. Tap ⊙ to either exclude or include these services and apps.

• Tap Excluded apps to see an app list of the excluded apps. Tap ＋ Add apps to select the apps to exclude from the memory usage checks.

Advanced device care options

There are other available device care features in the Advanced menu.

◌ Navigate to Settings > ◉ Battery and device care. The following options will be displayed:

- ◌ Search: Find the panels available for installation or are already installed.
- Care report: See the information about the charging, restart history, and temperature tips.
- ⋮ More options:
- Show icon on Apps screen: Show the icon for Device care on the Apps screen.
- Automation: Automatically optimize

your device at times set based on the pattern of your usage.

- Contact us: Utilize Samsung members to contact Samsung support.

- About Device care: See the license information and the Device care features.

Language and input

Configure your input settings and device's language.

Change the device language

You can add more languages to your language list and arrange them how you like. If an app is not compatible with your default language, then it will go to the next language in your list.

1. Navigate to Settings > ⚙ General management > Language.

2. Tap ➕ Add language, and choose a language from the list.

3. Tap Set as default to select another language for the device.

• To choose another language on the list, tap the language of choice, then tap Apply.

Text-to-speech

Set up the options for your Text-to-Speech (TTS). TTS is used for different accessibility features, like Voice Assistant.

○ Navigate to Settings > ⚙ General management > Text-to-speech for the following options:

- Preferred engine: Select either Google or Samsung's Text-to-speech engine. Tap ⚙ Settings for the options.
- Language: Choose the default speech-language.
- Speech rate: Configure the speed of the spoken text.
- Pitch: Set the speech's pitch.
- Play: Tap to play a short preview of speech synthesis.
- Reset: Reset the pitch's speech rate.

Keyboard list and default

Select your default keyboard, change the keyboard settings and modify the built-in keyboards.

Navigate to Settings > General management > Keyboard list and default to get the following options:

- Default keyboard: Select a default keyboard for your device's menus.
- Samsung keyboard: Modify the settings of the Samsung keyboard.
- Google voice typing: Modify the settings for the Google Voice input.
- Samsung voice input: Modify the settings for the Samsung voice input.
- Keyboard button on the navigation bar: Activate a button on the navigation bar to switch between keyboards.

Physical keyboards

Customize the options of your connected physical keyboard (sold separately).

1. Navigate to Settings > ⊜ General management.
2. Tap Physical keyboard, then select an option:
• Show on-screen keyboard: Display the on-screen keyboard when a physical keyboard is being used.
• Keyboard shortcuts: Display the keyboard shortcuts explanations on the screen.
• Change language shortcut: Disable or enable the shortcuts for the language key for your physical keyboard.

Mouse and trackpad

Configure the button assignment and pointer speed for an optional trackpad or mouse (not included).

- Navigate to Settings > ⊜ General management > Mouse and trackpad.
- Under the Pointer speed menu, drag the slider to the left for it to move slower or to the right, for it to go faster.
- Tap Primary mouse button, then select either Right or Left.

Autofill service

Make use of autofill service to save time while input your information.

1. Navigate to Settings > ⊜ General Management.

2. Tap Autofill service to see your selected service.

- To customize your service tap ⚙ Settings to customize.
- To change your default service, tap Autofill service.

Date and time

By default, your device receives time and date information from the wireless network. You can still set the time and date manually when you are outside the network coverage.

- Navigate to Settings > General management > Date and time. The following options will be displayed:
- Automatic date and time: Receive

time and date updates from your wireless network. When the Automatic date and time is disabled, the following options will be available:

- Select time zone: Select a new time zone.

- Set date: Input the current date.

- Set time: Input the current time.

• Use 24-hour format: Set the time display format.

Customization service

The Samsung devices, services and apps are made to provide you with customized contents by learning what you like in an intelligent and smart way.

The Samsung's Customization Service gives an improved user experience, including customized recommendations and content, based on your information obtained and the way you make use of Samsung's services.

- Navigate to Settings > General management > Customization service.

Troubleshooting

You can search for software updates and device reset services if necessary.

Software update

Search for and install the available device software updates. The options may differ by carrier.

- Navigate to Settings > Software update to get the following options:
  • Check for updates: Search for

software updates manually.

- Check for software updates: Search for software updates manually.
- Continue update: Resume an interrupted update.
- Show software update history: See a list of all your device software updates.
- Smart updates: Automatically install security updates.
- Use software update assistant: Connect your PC to your device to make use of the software update assistant tool.
- Download and install: Search for software updates and install any available one.
- Last update: See the information about the currently installed software.
- Update PRL: Download and install the update for your Preferred Roaming List.

- Update Profile: Update your user profile info automatically.
- UICC unlock: Activate the SIM slot to be compatible with another carrier's SIM card. For help, contact your carrier.

Reset

Reset network and device settings. You can also reset your device to its factory defaults.

Reset all settings

Resetting your device to its factory settings resets everything except the language, account settings and security. Your personal data will not be affected.

1. Navigate to Settings, > General management > Reset > Reset all settings.

2. Tap Reset settings, then confirm when prompted.

Reset network settings

With the Reset network settings, you can reset the mobile data, Bluetooth, and Wi-Fi settings.

1. Navigate to Settings > General management > Reset > Reset network settings.

2. Tap Reset settings, then confirm when prompted.

Reset accessibility settings

You can reset the accessibility settings of your device. The accessibility settings of your personal data and downloaded apps will not be affected.

1. Navigate to Settings > General management > Reset > Reset accessibility settings.
2. Tap Reset settings, then confirm when prompted.

Auto restart at set times

Set your device to reset automatically at scheduled times. Any data that is not saved will be lost during a restart.

1. Navigate to Settings > General management > Reset > Auto restart at

set times.

2. Tap ⬤ to activate Auto restart, then assign the following parameters:

- Days: Choose the day of the week to restart your device automatically.
- Time: Set the time to restart your device.

Factory Data Reset

You can erase all your device data by resetting your device to factory defaults.

Doing this permanently deletes all your device data include downloaded apps, application and system data settings, the settings for Google and other accounts, your pictures, music, videos, and other files.

The Factory Reset Protection (FRP) will be activated when you sign into a Google Account. This protects your device data if your device is either stolen or lost. If your factory reset your device with an activated FRP feature, then you must input your Google account's password and username before you can regain access to the device. Without the right credentials, you cannot access the device.

☼ Note that it can take up to 24 hours for your password to be synced to all the devices with your registered account if you reset your Google Account password.

Before you reset your device:

1. Ascertain that your info to be kept has been transferred to the storage area.

2. Log in to your Google Account and verify your password and user name. To reset your device:

1. Navigate to Settings > General management > Reset > Factory data reset.

2. Tap Reset then follow the prompts to perform the reset.

3. Follow the displayed prompt when the device restarts to configure your device.

Factory Reset Protection

Factory Reset Protection will be activated when you sign into a Google Account on your device.

This feature restricts the usage of your phone by other people if it has been reset without your permission. As an instance, if your device gets stolen and a factory reset is performed on it, only someone that has your Google Account password and username can have access to the device.

You will not be able to make use of your device after performing a factory data reset if you do not have your Google password and username.

Warning: Before you send your device to a Samsung- authorized service center, erase the Google Account and perform a factory data reset.

Activate Factory Reset Protection

When you add a Google Account to your device, the FRP security feature will be automatically activated.

Disable Factory Reset Protection

To disable FRP, erase all your Google Accounts from the device.

1. Navigate to Settings > ⚙ Accounts and backup > Manage accounts > [Google Account].
2. Tap Remove account.

Collect diagnostics

Gather diagnostic data for troubleshooting. This option may vary by carrier.

○ Navigate to Settings > 🔄 General management > Reset > Collect diagnostics. You can choose from the following options:

- Device data collection: Help device troubleshooting.

Chapter 22: Accessibility

There are accessibility settings for those with hearing, seeing, or other issues. The accessibility services are special features that make the device easier to be used by everyone.

Recommended for you

See the list of accessibility features which you are making use of and other recommended features that you may like.

- Navigate to Settings > 	 Accessibility > Recommended for you to view recommendations.

TalkBack

Make use of special settings and controls for navigation without making use of the screen.

1. Navigate to Settings > 👤 Accessibility > TalkBack.

2. Tap ⬤ to activate this feature then tap an option to customize:

• TalkBack shortcut: Quickly switch on TalkBack by selecting a shortcut.

• Settings: Set up the TalkBack settings to assist you better.

Visibility enhancements

You can set up the Accessibility features to help you with the visual aspects of your device.

Clarity and Colors

For easier viewing, you can adjust the

text contrast and colors, and other screen elements.

○ Navigate to Settings > ⊕ Accessibility > Visibility enhancements and tap an option:

• High contrast theme: For easier viewing, adjust the screen fonts and colors to increase the contrast.

• High contrast fonts: Adjust the font outline and color to increase the background contrast.

• High contrast keyboard: Adjust the Samsung keyboard size and change its colors to increase the contrast between the background and the keys.

• Highlight buttons: Display the buttons with shaded backgrounds to make them have a better display against the wallpaper.

- Color inversion: Reverse the color display from white text on a black background to black text on a white background.
- Color adjustment: Adjust the screen color if you find it hard to see some colors.
- Add color filter: Adjust the colors of the screen if you experience difficulty in reading the text.
- Remove animations: Erase certain screen effects if you are motion-sensitive.

Zoom and Size

You can create shortcuts for accessibility features and increase the supported screen element sizes.

○ Navigate to Settings > Accessibility

> Visibility enhancements and tap any of the following options:

- Magnifier window: Magnify screen-displayed contents.
- Magnification: Use exaggerated gestures including, double pinching triple-tapping, and dragging two fingers across the screen.
- Large mouse/touchpad pointer: Make use of a large pointer for a connected touchpad or mouse (accessories not included).
- Font size and style: Configure the screen fonts.
- Screen zoom: Configure the level of the screen zoom.

Hearing enhancements

You can set up the Accessibility features to aid with the device's audio aspects.

This options may differ by carrier.

Sounds

You can adjust the quality of the audio when using earphones or hearing aids.

⚬ Navigate to Settings > 🧍 Accessibility > Hearing enhancements and tap any of the following option:

- Real time text: Enable the real-time text (RTT) calling.
- Hearing aid support: Enhance the quality of sound to function better with hearing aids.
- Amplify ambient sound: Activate this feature and connect headphones to your device to magnify the conversation sounds.
- Adapt sound: Configure each ear's sound for a better listening experience.

- Left/right sound balance: Make use of the slider to adjust the right and left balance when listening to stereo options
- Mono audio: Switch the audio to mono from stereo when making use of one earphone.
- Mute all sounds: For your privacy, turn off all audio and notifications.

Text display

You can see closed captions when viewing multimedia and also convert speech to text.

○ Navigate to Settings > 🧍 Accessibility > Hearing enhancements and tap any of the options:
- Live Transcribe: Make use of the

microphone to record speeches and convert them to text.

- Live Caption: Automatically caption the speeches in the media you are playing on your device.
- Google subtitles (CC): Setup the subtitle and closed caption services.
- Sound notifications: Get notified when the device detects a doorbell or a baby crying.

Dexterity and Interaction

You can set up Accessibility features to aid with limited dexterity when having interactions with your device.

Alternate input

You can control your device using several control and input methods kinds of inputs and controls.

○ Navigate to Settings > 🛉 Accessibility > Interaction and dexterity then tap any of the following options:

- Universal switch: Use your customized switches to control your device.

- Assistant menu: Improve the device accessibility for users having reduced dexterity.

Interactions

You can streamline the motions needed to respond to alarms and notifications and receive phone calls.

○ Navigate to Settings > 🛉 Accessibility

> Interaction and dexterity and tap any of the following options:

- Answering and ending calls:

‐ Read caller names aloud: Listen to the names of callers being read aloud when using headsets (sold separately) or Bluetooth.

‐ Answer automatically: Receive calls after a set time when making use of headsets (sold separately) or Bluetooth.

‐ Press Volume up to answer: Answer calls using the Volume keys.

‐ Press Side key to end calls: Press the Side Key to end calls.

- Interaction control: Customize the keyboards, hard keys, and screen interaction areas.

Touch settings

You can configure your screen to be less sensitive to touch and taps.

○   Navigate to Settings > ⓘ Accessibility > Interaction and dexterity then tap any of the following options:

•   Touch and hold delay: Choose an interval of time for this action.

•   Tap duration: Set the length of time that an interaction will be held to be understood as a tap.

•   Ignore repeated touches: Set a time frame for repeated touches to be ignored.

Mouse and physical keyboard

Set up the settings for a connected

physical keyboard and mouse.

○   Navigate to Settings > 🯆 Accessibility > Interaction and dexterity and tap any of the following options:

• Auto click after pointer stops: Automatically select an item when the pointer stops on it.

• Sticky keys: The key stays down when you press a modifier key like Shift, Ctrl, Shift. This allows you to press keyboard shortcuts one key at a time.

• Slow keys: Set the length of time that a key must be held before it will be recognized as a press. This helps you to avoid accidental key presses.

• Bounce keys: Set how the length of time to wait before the second press of the same key can be accepted. This helps you to avoid pressing the same key many times accidentally.

Advanced settings

You can customize more accessibility services and features for your device.

💡 You can download more accessibility apps from the Google Play store.

Accessibility shortcuts

○ Navigate to Settings > 🯅 Accessibility > Advanced settings and tap any of the following options:

• Accessibility button: Select an accessibility shortcut for the Accessibility button.

• Side and Volume up keys: Set up

which selected Accessibility features to open by quickly pressing the Volume up and Side and keys together.

• Volume up and down keys: Setup the selected services to switch on when you hold down the Volume down and Volume up keys for three seconds.

Notifications

◌ Navigate to Settings > 🯈 Accessibility > Advanced settings and tap any of the following options:

• Flash notification: Flash either the screen or camera light when an alarm sounds or when you receive notifications.

• Time to take action: Select the length of time to display messages that request you to take action, but are only temporarily visible (like notifications).

- Speak keyboard input aloud: What you type on the keyboard will be read aloud by the device.
- Bixby Vision for accessibility: Add the modes to describe scenes, read text aloud, detect colors, and more.

- Voice Label: Write the NFC tags' voice recordings to give you information about locations or objects as you get closer to them.

Installed services

You can install more device assistance services.

○ Navigate to Settings > 🧑 Accessibility > Installed services.

💡 Note that after you have installed the additional accessibility services, they will be configured and listed here.

About Accessibility

The license and legal information of the current Accessibility software are present in Settings.

○ Go to Settings > ⊛ Accessibility > About Accessibility. The following information is displayed there:

• Version: See the current Accessibility software version.

• Open source licenses: See the open source license information that Accessibility uses.

Chapter 23: Edge panels

On the Edge panels are different customizable panels that you can access from the screen's edge. The Edge panels can be used to see contacts, apps, news, sports, tasks and other info.

Apps panel

In a two-column arrangement, you can add apps in the Apps panel.

1. From any part of the screen, drag the Edge handle to the screen's center, then swipe till the Apps panel is seen.
2. To open, tap any app or app pair shortcut. You can also tap ⁞⁞All apps to get the full list of apps.

- To open more windows in the pop-up view, drag the icon of an app to the open screen from the Apps panel.

To setup the Apps panel:

1. Drag the Edge handle to the screen's center from any part of the screen, then swipe till the Apps panel is seen.

2. Tap Edit panel to add include more apps to the Apps panel.

- To place an app in the Apps panel, look for it on the screen's left side and then tap on it to include it in an available space on the right column.
- To create a shortcut to a folder, drag an app from the screen's left side, at the

upside of an app in the right columns.

- To change the app's order on the panel, drag each app to your preferred location.

- To delete an app, tap ⊖ Remove.

3. Tap ⟨ Back to save the changes.

Configure Edge panels

You can configure the Edge panels.

1. Navigate to Edge screen > ⚙ Settings.

2. The following options are present:

- ⊙ Checkbox: Disable or enable the panels.

- Edit (if available): Configure the individual panels.

- 🔍 Search: Look for the panels that

are either available for installation or have been installed.

- ⋮ More options:

  - Reorder: Drag the panels to the right or left to change their orders.

  - Hide on Lock screen: Select the panels to be hidden on the Lock screen anytime the secure lock is activated.

- Galaxy Store: Look for and download more Edge panels from the Galaxy Store.

3. Tap ⟨ Back to save the changes.

Edge panel style and position

You can change the Edge handle's positioning position.

○ To see the following options, navigate to Settings > ⊙ Display > Edge panels >

Handle:

- Edge handle: Drag it to change the Edge handle's positioning along the screen's edge.
- Position: Select the side where the Edge screen will display on, either Left or Right.
- Lock handle position: Activate this to stop the handle position from moving when it is held and touched.
- Style: Select an Edge handle color.
- Transparency: Adjust the Edge handle's transparency by dragging the slider.
- Size: Adjust the Edge handle's size by dragging the slider.

About Edge panels

You can see the Edge panel's license info and the current software version.

○ Go to Settings, then ⚙ Display > Edge panels > About Edge panels.

Index

A

Accessibility, 150, 305, 306, 307, 308, 309, 310, 311, 312, 313, 315, 316, 317, 318, 319, 320
Advanced settings, 143, 236, 237, 317, 318
Airplane mode, 201
Always On Display, 44, 48, 49, 50, 247, 255, 256, 257, 282
App icons, 27
AR Zone, 80, 159

B

Biometric security, 62, 253
Bixby, 10, 11, 75, 80, 173, 319
Bluetooth, 116, 195, 196, 197, 198, 201, 212, 224, 232, 271, 297, 314

C

Calculator, 84
Calendar, 85, 86, 87, 88
Camera, 154, 155, 156, 159, 160, 161, 162, 163, 164, 165, 166, 171, 172, 229
Chrome, 61, 146
Clock, 49, 50, 88, 89, 90, 91, 92, 93, 94, 95, 256
Connect to a printer, 213
Connections, 189, 190, 191, 194, 195, 196, 197, 199, 200, 201, 202, 204, 205, 206, 207, 208, 210, 211, 212, 213, 214, 215, 216, 217, 218
Contacts, 96, 97, 99, 100, 101, 102, 103, 104, 105, 113, 122, 142

D

Data usage, 204, 205, 206, 207, 208
DeX, 69, 151, 152
Digital wellbeing, 46
Display, 24, 25, 35, 44, 49, 50, 91, 98, 127, 170, 182, 237, 240, 241, 242,

244, 245, 246, 247, 248, 249, 254, 255, 256, 257, 282, 290, 324, 326
Drive, 146, 277

E

Easy mode, 35
Edge panels, 321, 323, 324, 326
enhancements, 309, 310, 311
Enter text, 51

F

Face recognition, 62, 63, 64, 110
Fingerprint scanner, 66, 111

G

Galaxy Store, 71, 77, 79, 81, 83, 244, 324
Gallery, 28, 29, 162, 173, 174, 176, 177, 179, 180
Game Launcher, 81
Gmail, 147
Google, 11, 12, 42, 48, 61, 71, 77, 79, 83, 146, 147, 148, 249, 257, 258, 274, 277, 278, 288, 289, 299, 300, 301, 302, 303, 312, 317

H

Home screen settings, 33

I

images, 28, 70, 131, 143, 157, 160, 161, 168, 173, 179, 180, 213, 247
Internet, 61, 106, 107, 108, 109, 110, 111, 212

L

LinkedIn, 78

M

Maps, 148
Messages, 70, 140, 142
Microsoft apps, 77
Mobile continuity, 69
Mobile hotspot, 208, 209, 210, 211, 212
Mobile networks, 201, 202
Multi window, 185
My Files, 143, 144, 145

N

Navigation, 17, 24, 25, 31, 51, 85, 86, 135, 228
Nearby device scanning, 213

Notification, 35, 37, 39, 40, 41, 117, 198, 222, 226, 233, 234, 237, 238, 254

O

Office, 78
OneDrive, 78
Outlook, 13, 78

P

parental controls, 46
Phone, 13, 61, 112, 113, 117, 118, 119, 120, 121, 122, 123, 124, 126, 127, 197
Photos, 70, 148, 249
pictures, 29, 70, 140, 141, 148, 155, 156, 157, 160, 161, 162, 168, 170, 173, 174, 176, 179, 229, 249, 299
Play Movies & TV, 148
Play Store, 77, 83, 148
Play video, 176, 177

R

Record videos, 158, 163, 169, 171
recorder, 182, 183, 184
Remove an account, 275

S

Samsung Health, 128
Samsung Notes, 44, 131, 132, 134, 135
Samsung Pay, 136, 137, 138, 139, 200
Scene optimizer, 160, 167
screenshot, 180, 181, 182
shooting mode, 155, 156, 161, 166, 171
Side key, 6, 7, 10, 11, 141, 142, 154, 250, 314
Side key settings, 10
Single take, 156, 161
SmartThings, 42, 83
Space Zoom, 162

T

Tethering, 212
Themes, 29, 30, 31, 51

V

Video enhancer, 177
videos, 8, 28, 29, 53, 78, 143, 148, 149, 157, 158, 160, 161, 163, 164, 169, 170, 173, 176, 177, 178, 179, 180, 230, 299
View pictures, 173
Visibility

enhancements, 306, 307, 309
voicemail, 13, 114, 115, 119, 120, 122

W

Wallpaper, 28, 29, 256
Widgets, 31, 32, 256
Wi-Fi, 7, 8, 189, 190, 191, 192, 193, 194, 201, 204, 206, 207, 208, 209, 213, 261, 270, 271, 297
Windows, 69, 70, 149, 150

Y

YouTube, 53, 149
YT Music, 149

Manufactured by Amazon.ca
Bolton, ON